UNDERSTANDING

EQUINE BUSINESS
BASICS

YOUR **GUIDE** TO HORSE HEALTH
CARE AND MANAGEMENT

Copyright © 2001 The Blood-Horse, Inc.

All Rights reserved. No part of this book may be repro-
duced in any form by any means, including photocopying,
audio recording, or any information storage or retrieval system, without the permission in writing from the copyright
holder. Inquiries should be addressed to Publisher, The
Blood-Horse, Inc., Box 4038, Lexington, KY 40544-4038.

ISBN 1-58150-063-7

Printed in the United States of America

First Edition: May 2001

1 2 3 4 5 6 7 8 9 10

UNDERSTANDING

EQUINE BUSINESS BASICS

YOUR **GUIDE** TO HORSE HEALTH
CARE AND MANAGEMENT

By Milton C. Toby and Karen L. Perch, Ph.D.

The Blood-Horse, Inc. Lexington, KY

Contents

INTRODUCTION

Pursuit of any business activity involving horses comes with a built-in dilemma: horses are supposed to be fun; running a business generally is not. Faced with a choice between watching a new foal frolic in the field and dealing with a troublesome employee, balancing the books, paying the bills, or any of the hundred other jobs necessary to keep a business running, the preference is clear.

It is tempting to sit back on the porch and watch the new crop of foals, in the process putting the business tasks aside for another time. Eventually, though, the employee problems must be addressed, the books must be balanced, the bills must be paid. The purpose of this book is not to make these business tasks fun. If we could manage that trick, we might be writing this book from a retirement villa in the south of France or from a condo next to a Pebble Beach fairway.

Our goals, instead, are more modest. The following chapters are not intended to be exhaustive treatises on any of the subjects addressed, and, as much as we would like to, we cannot offer absolute solutions to any of your specific problems. We hope this book will highlight and clarify some areas of concern in your business, though, and possibly bring to your attention some topics that you might not have considered. And we hope that by identifying potential problem areas in your business and by pointing you toward some possible solutions or resources, we can help you deal efficiently with those necessary, but clearly less-than-fun portions of your horse business.

A recurring theme throughout the following pages is the realization that you cannot be an expert in everything, and that the success of your horse enterprise may depend on the team of professionals you assemble to help you reach your goals. Some of these business relationships are obvious, some are not.

You certainly need a sound working relationship with a good veterinarian and farrier. Just as necessary to your success may be an attorney versed in equine law to review contracts and other documents; an accountant to assist with bookkeeping, payroll, and tax filings; a banker with experience in horse-related activities to help you with financing purchases of horses, equipment, and land, and establishing a line of credit to smooth out seasonal fluctuations in income; and state and county extension professionals.

National, state, and local breed associations and saddle clubs also can be valuable sources of both information and support. Other valuable resources are organizations aimed at small businesses in general, such as the Service Corps of Retired Executives (SCORE) and the Small Business Administration (SBA).

In other words, you are not alone. No matter how vexing a problem appears, odds are that someone else has been in the same situation, and you should build on his or her expertise. Identifying this common ground is one of the purposes of this book.

Finally, a caveat: Laws vary from jurisdiction to jurisdiction, and what works — or is legal — in one state may not apply at all in another. While we have tried to keep specific legal references to a minimum, at times this was impossible. Unless otherwise identified, laws, statutes, and regulations referred to here are either federal or specific to Kentucky, where we are licensed to practice law. Questions about application of legal or business principles identified in the following pages should be addressed to a professional knowledgeable about the horse business and about the law in your particular state.

Just as this book is not intended to replace the services of a professional familiar with your business and your state laws, it is not intended to be comprehensive about any particular subject. By necessity, we have been selective about the general topics to be covered and about the treatment of these topics.

Various ways to own your business, whether sole proprietorship, partnership, or corporation, are discussed in Chapter 1, along with some bookkeeping basics.

We cannot tell you everything about balance sheets, profit and loss statements, cash flow projections, and budgets in a few pages, but we can stress the importance of sound accounting to the success of your horse business. The types of records you should keep, including records of transactions, payroll, legal documents that establish the nature of your business, and estate planning records are addressed in Chapter 2.

Ask anyone about the most difficult aspect of his or her horse business, and the likely answer will be finding and keeping good workers. Chapter 3 takes you though the basics of employer-employee relationships, including employment contracts, discrimination and sexual harassment, worker's compensation, minimum wage, workplace safety, and employing foreign nationals. Chapter 4 deals with the ins and outs of buying and selling, specifically some of the implications of the Uniform Commercial Code for horse sales.

If you are lucky enough to make money with your horse business, or even if you are not, Chapter 5 provides some insight into taxes. While it probably is impossible to eliminate taxes altogether, it may be possible to make your taxes predictable, a situation that might be the next best thing. Protecting your assets with insurance is covered in Chapter

6, and various ways to settle disputes outside the courtroom, collectively known as alternative dispute resolution, is covered in Chapter 7. Finally, Chapter 8 offers some valuable resources for anyone in the horse business.

Some areas of interest, such as dealing with the 45-50 pounds of manure each of your horses produces every day, are better suited to a discussion of farm-management practices. By the same token, we did not address bankruptcy, not because horse farms never get into financial trouble, but because the bankruptcy laws are in a state of flux, and anything we might say likely would be outdated by the time you read it. The same is true with estate taxes, an area in which the law is changing. You should consult an attorney for the most current information. Other topics covered in our earlier book, *Understanding Equine Law*, are not repeated here.

We hope you find the following useful.

Milton C. Toby, J.D.
Karen L. Perch, Ph.D., J.D.
Attorneys at Law
Lexington, Kentucky

CHAPTER 1

How You Own Your Business Affects Your Responsibilities

The forms of ownership available to you as a horse business owner include sole proprietorship, some form of corporation, or some form of partnership. The form you choose will affect your personal responsibilities to taxing authorities and to others.

Ideally, you should talk to a tax accountant and an attorney before you begin your business. These people will serve as advisers only and will not assume any responsibility or liability for any part of your horse business. Nor will they help manage the business, unless specifically hired to do so. You may add other advisers as you decide how you will own your business.

If you already have an ongoing business, you may want to schedule a meeting with your advisers to discuss some of the available options. In many circumstances, you may also have a business manager who makes short-term and long-term planning decisions and also participates in day-to-day operational decisions.

If, after discussing the matter with your advisers, you choose to operate your business as a sole proprietor, you are ultimately responsible for everything. As the only owner of the business, you may be the only manager of day-to-day activities, though you may employ others to assist you. You pay any income tax due and report all income and losses on your individual income tax return.

When you die, assuming you still own your business at your death, the value of the business will be part of your personal estate and may be subject to inheritance or estate tax. You have personal responsibility for any debts and any harm or damage to others or to their property that occurs as a result of operation of your horse business. By going it alone, however, you don't have to share your business affairs with anyone other than taxing authorities and potential lenders. You make all the management decisions.

AT A GLANCE

• Talk to an attorney or accountant before starting an equine business.

• Several ownership options exist, including a sole proprietorship and various types of partnerships.

• One of the first business management decisions you must make is whether to use the cash or accrual method of accounting.

You can include a few more people in your horse business and your planning and management teams by electing to own it as an "S" corporation rather than as a sole proprietorship. You must meet the strict technical requirements of the Internal Revenue Service in order to qualify.

This form of ownership limits somewhat your potential personal liabilities and can ensure a smooth transition of the business upon your death, but shareholders in the business will still report income and losses on their individual tax returns. More people will have detailed information about how the business is doing financially. Someone must have the responsibility for the record keeping and reporting. It could be you or someone else on the management team.

With the form of business generally known as a "C" corporation, you can have as many shareholders as you want. In a sense, each shareholder becomes a member of your ongoing business management team and must receive full information about the financial affairs of your horse business. Shareholders often get to vote, so you don't make the business management decisions by yourself.

The trade-off for shared management decisions is that you generally have no personal liability for debts of the business or for harm or injury caused as a result of operation of the business. This can be either an advantage or a disadvantage depending upon how you like to do business and how much privacy you want. If your horse business is a "C" corporation, it must also pay its own income taxes. This can be a distinct disadvantage for the owner of a small horse-business operation. Be sure to talk to your attorney and accountant before selecting this form of ownership!

For tax and other purposes, a partnership is essentially a group of taxpayers who have joined together to pursue some common business interest. If you form a partnership, each general partner is part of the business management team, though you can assign particular responsibilities to various partners.

Typically, each general partner is responsible for all the debts and other obligations of the partnership. Suppose, for example, that you and three other people join together to form a horse boarding business. You intend to share equally in all expenses and income of the business. You decide, as a partnership, to borrow money to build an additional barn. If the business doesn't generate enough income to repay the debt, the general partners are all liable for the amount owed, and you can expect each partner to contribute an equal amount to retire the debt.

If, however, one partner does not meet his obligations to the partnership, the remaining three are liable for the entire outstanding debt.

Limited partners do not become part of the business management team and do not assume responsibility for the affairs or liabilities of the partnership beyond the amount of their investment.

As you can see, a partnership is not something in which you should engage without first discussing the advantages and disadvantages to your particular horse business with your initial planning team. Get advice before you begin your horse business.

BOOKKEEPING BASICS

After you decide who the management team is, based upon how you own your business, you will need to address quickly one aspect of business management that many business people dislike — accounting issues. No, you don't want to be an accountant, and this book will not turn you into one. Unless your horse business is large enough to employ a bookkeeper, some member of the business management team will have to be assigned the responsibility for record keeping and financial reporting.

Even if you use an accountant to prepare tax returns, that person must have financial information in a usable form. In addition, someone in your management team must be able to discuss with the accountant decisions that the business managers and owners have made. If you intend to prepare tax returns without the use of an accountant, it becomes even more critical to understand certain basic terminology.

You will need to be able to prepare and read financial statements so that you can compare how your horse business is doing from year to year. This will enable you to see what your business has accomplished and assist you in planning for the future. The discussion that follows is intended to give you some of the information you will need.

CHOOSE YOUR ACCOUNTING METHOD

Generally speaking, accounting is just a way to record financial transactions. One of the first business management decisions you must make is whether to use the cash method or the accrual method of accounting. The cash method of accounting is familiar to most people. Individual taxpayers, for example, use the cash method of accounting. They report income to the Internal Revenue Service, as a general rule, in the year in which it is earned and claim allowable deductions in the year in which the expenses occur.

Professional service businesses and other small firms that maintain no inventory and have few long-term assets also use this method of accounting. In order to qualify for the cash method of accounting, however, the business cannot be one that requires an inventory. You must use the cash method unless you keep account books.

With the accrual method of accounting, you report income when you earn it, even if you do not get paid during the tax year. You report expenses when you incur them, even if you do not pay them during the tax year. If you sell equipment or supplies as part of your horse business, you may be required to use the accrual method of accounting, which means you would also be required to keep account books. To help you understand the practical differences between the cash and accrual methods, consider the example of Peter Green.

Peter Green owns a 300-acre farm on which he boards horses, maintains riding trails for use by the public, and offers horseback riding lessons. He likes his privacy, and the only partner of any kind that he wants is his wife, Mary. She helps with the books. He has chosen to operate as a sole proprietor.

Existing contracts for the year total $12,000, with various beginning and ending dates. Most people, but not all, pay these monthly. A few people paid in lump sums at the beginning of their contracts, with those contracts totaling $4,000. This was a rare treat for Mr. Green, but he certainly needed the money and welcomed the unexpected and unusual security this gave him.

In addition, a new boarder has just signed a one-year contract to keep her horse on the farm, with monthly payments over the 12-month period. That contract will expire next year. One doting grandparent gave a year of weekly riding lessons as a birthday gift to her grandchild this year and paid for the lessons all at once. Plus, Mr. Green expects to earn about $6,000 from the extensive riding trails he has developed on the farm.

Mr. Green has had a difficult time, despite having a valid contract, collecting for veterinarian expenses he incurred in an emergency situation on behalf of a horse owner. Another customer had not paid all of her boarding fees and was in arrears when she moved her horse to another stable. He has decided to write off the losses as bad debts rather than pursue them in court. He has had various other ordinary business expenses totaling $3,600 so far this year.

As a sole proprietor, Mr. Green simply includes business income and expense and loss information on Schedule C of the federal form 1040 income tax return. So, what difference does it make if he uses the cash method or the accrual method of accounting? Let's see.

On the facts given here, let's assume first that Mr. Green uses the cash method of accounting. With this method, Mr. Green will claim as income on Schedule C all of the income from the existing contracts, riding lessons, and use of riding trails that he actually receives this year. If he doesn't receive part of it until next year, then he will not report the income until then. He will report as income the full $4,000 lump sum payments for boarding contracts as well as the money received from the grandparent because he received it this year.

He may claim as expenses the regular operating expenses, which are $3,600 so far this year. The bad debt is another matter, however. He can only write off as a bad debt those items that were from sales or services previously included in income and definitely known to be worthless. Mr. Green would have to meet very strict requirements of the Internal Revenue Service in order to satisfy these criteria. As a cash-basis taxpayer, it is more difficult for him to do this. If he doesn't pursue all his legal remedies, he does not know the debt to be worthless.

If Mr. Green chooses the accrual method of accounting, on the other hand, several things will be different. Although he received $4,000 in lump-sum boarding contracts, he doesn't actually earn the money until the horses are boarded for the week or month. The one-time payment from the grandparent, likewise, is not earned until the lessons are given. Mr. Green can defer reporting these as income until they are earned. This lowers his taxable income for the current year. Whether he can claim the bad debt is unclear.

With respect to the boarding fees that were in arrears, as an accrual method taxpayer he probably claimed the boarding fees when they were due, which would satisfy the first part of the test. He must still be able to demonstrate to the satisfaction of the Internal Revenue Service that the debt is worthless.

For Mr. Green, even as a sole proprietor, the accrual method of accounting may give some tax benefit not available to cash-basis taxpayers. The greater the complexity of the business, in terms of numbers of owners, form of ownership chosen, etc., the more likely the accrual method will be of tax benefit. Remember, however, that the accrual method requires that account books be kept.

Formal records and careful documentation are necessities. Perhaps because it is less familiar to most individuals, business owners sometimes improperly record the timing of income and expenses. The cash method, while still requiring good records, is simpler. You cannot change accounting method from year to year in an attempt to lower your tax bill. Once you have begun your business and filed your first income tax return, you must get permission from the Internal Revenue Service to change your accounting method. Ask your accountant for advice before you start!

USE COMMON FINANCIAL REPORTS TO YOUR ADVANTAGE

One of the reasons for generating financial reports is obviously to document income and expenses for tax-reporting purposes. Some horse businesses also may have to worry about sales taxes, especially in states where such taxes are imposed on services. Equally important, however, and frequently overlooked is the benefit of having good financial reports for planning the direction of your horse business.

BALANCE SHEETS GIVE A PHOTOGRAPH OF YOUR BUSINESS

The balance sheet provides a simple snapshot of the company at a given point in time. Sometimes it is referred to as a net worth statement. The first part of the balance sheet lists the assets or resources of the business. Assets include cash and property treated as cash, such as checking and savings accounts, certificates of deposit, etc., as well as the value of property and equipment. Accounts receivable are also assets, but these may not appear on the balance sheets of cash-basis taxpayers.

The second part of the balance sheet contains a list of business liabilities and owner equity in the business. Liabilities generally include accounts payable or bills due as of the date of the document, taxes due, and debt. Owner equity is a combination of capital contributions made by owners and undistributed earnings.

Take a look at the Green Farm balance sheet included at the end of this chapter. After consulting with his accountant and attorney, he decided to consider his entire farm part of the business. Although he recently added the riding trails and horseback riding lessons, he has not started separate businesses for these activities. He is using a calendar year. Notice that the balance sheet is "as of" a particular date. As a sole proprietor, Mr. Green wants to keep things simple, but he could provide even more detail by specifying the various accounts in which he has his funds and by distinguishing current assets and liabilities from non-current assets and liabilities. Current assets are those that will be received as cash or converted to cash within one year. Current liabilities are those that are due and payable within one year. Everything else is non-current.

As sole proprietor, Mr. Green's year-end equity equals the net worth of the horse-farm operation. You will notice that the total liabilities and equity equals total assets. This is always the case. If Mr. Green had partners or shareholders, he would have to calculate the equity for each one. Each owner's equity is that owner's opening balance equity, plus his or her investments during the year, less any distributions made during the year to that owner. The totals of the liabilities plus the total equity of all owners will always equal the total value of the assets, just as it does for Mr. Green as shown in the example.

Because Mr. Green has chosen to plow his net ordinary income back into the business and because he is a sole proprietor, it appears as part of his equity. If he had taken some of the earnings for family living expenses, that amount would appear as a reduction in his equity.

PROFIT AND LOSS STATEMENTS GAUGE YOUR PROGRESS

The profit and loss statement, sometimes called a P&L or even an income statement, shows the net earnings of a business over a specific period. The standard period is one year, though the year may be tied to something other than a calendar. The fiscal year for your business might be tied to the date on which your business began or to a key time in your business. For example, a horse breeder might tie the end of a fiscal year to the completion of yearling sales held each year so that all revenues received from the sales fall in a particular reporting period.

Unlike the balance sheet, which is a statement of the net worth of the business at a particular point in time, the profit and loss statement tells a business owner if the business has increased or decreased over time. The profit and loss statement shows a summary of the income from all sources and the expenses by each category of expense. After subtracting the expenses paid or credited during the period from the income received or earned during the period, you will see your business' net income for the period reflected by the statement.

After you have been in business for more than one year, you can compare income and expenses from year to year using the profit and loss statement. You can track the sources of your income to see if, for example, your income from any particular source is increasing or decreasing as a percentage of your total income. You can see if expenses are as expected or if one or more categories are much more or much less than anticipated. This information can be helpful in planning for the next year. The Green Farm profit and loss statement gives you an example of how a simple document might look.

An examination of the Green Farm profit and loss statement (also at the end of the chapter) for the years 1999 and 2000 shows that income from general farming operations decreased while income from other areas increased. Mr. Green should ask himself whether this was intended or if he needs to make changes, such as hiring additional help for either the new areas or the general farm operations. He also should look at the expense items. Were they as expected? Should some of the items in the miscellaneous expense category be listed separately? Should a category be further reduced to increase net income? Should a category be increased or added to assist in the production of net income?

USE CASH FLOW PROJECTIONS TO ANTICIPATE CASH NEEDS

A cash-flow projection is strictly that — a forecast based upon assumptions you have made of the cash expected or needed at some time in the future. The purpose of a cash-flow projection is not to set targets or goals for the business but to anticipate cash needs. It should be revised as often as necessary, and even if you have a tendency to be optimistic, force yourself to be just a little pessimistic in making your projections.

Money that is owed to your horse business may never arrive, even from a customer with a good track record for paying on time. Expenses to renovate your barn may be larger than you expected. To make matters worse, when doing cash planning, you may even need to consider some things that do not even show up on your balance sheet. If you are using the cash method of accounting, for example, an order for feed will not appear on the balance sheet until you have paid for it.

An executory contract, one in which you have agreed to do something in the future, such as breeding a horse, may not appear in the balance sheet until money changes hands. A pending lawsuit in which your business may become liable for payment of money will be necessary to include in your cash-flow forecast, but will not appear in your balance sheet. An example of this might be a claim for negligence that an injured rider has made against your business. You might suddenly need cash if the jury decides your business was at fault.

In the case of poor Mr. Green, his cash-flow chart shows that he will not make it through the winter without careful advance planning. If his assumptions about the first three months of the year are reasonably correct, he needs to be sure to have savings on hand or a line of credit upon which he can draw until that time of year when his revenues exceed his expenses. Let's hope he has planned for everything!

DEVELOP A BUDGET

All businesses need a budget. All businesses need a budget. All businesses need a budget. Get the point? Few people really enjoy developing a budget because it is often perceived as some sort of straitjacket to prevent creativity or because it is based upon unrealistic goals. Such a budget is badly designed or poorly implemented. Your balance sheet and profit and loss statements tell you something about where your horse business has been and what it has already done. Your budget helps you take control of the future.

A well-conceived budget helps you get your business where you want it to go. It spells out the goals, breaks them into manageable pieces, allocates resources, and assigns responsibility for performance of various aspects of it. The written budget does not need to be elaborate, but should specify the period to be covered by the budget. It should clearly state the goals for which resources are being allocated. If goals will take longer than the budget period to be accomplished, the budget should state what part will be accomplished during the budgeted time period. Whenever possible, specific individuals should be assigned to complete tasks that will promote accomplishment of the goals.

In small horse businesses, a properly developed budget may be used primarily as a road map for attaining goals. In larger businesses, it also may be used for control of expenditures. In both situations, short-term or long-term goals are broken into chunks that can be accomplished within a given time period. The goals are prioritized, and resources are then allocated to goals in accordance with the priorities. When looking at the Green Farm profit and loss statement, it is clear that income from general farming has declined from 1999 to 2000. If this was the result of a decision by Mr. Green to commit fewer resources to general farm operations in hopes of increasing income from the other three areas, then he may not need to worry that net income as a whole also declined. He should ask, however, if the goals he set for his horse business were reasonable. If they were not, then he should use that information to revise his budget for the next time period.

The cash-flow projection also gives Mr. Green a picture, based upon assumptions that he hopes are realistic, about the cash flowing in and out of his business during a particular time frame. If all goes well, the items of outgoing cash are previously budgeted items for which Mr. Green is amply prepared. If so, that is one indication that the budget was realistic. If some items on the cash-flow projection were not bud-geted at all or if an item is much higher or lower than expect-ed, then either the assumptions that went into the cash flow were wrong or the budget was unrealistic or both.

DEVISE A SYSTEM OF INTERNAL CONTROL

As a business owner, you need some sort of system to prevent and detect errors in the recording of information about your business. It might be as simple as always paying bills and expenses by check, then reconciling the check reg-ister to the statement you receive from the bank each month. You might add to that recording expenses in a separate ledger, using receipts as your guide, and comparing the bal-ances in the checkbook. Take steps to physically safeguard your records so that in the event they are needed for a tax audit or to prove the terms of a contract, you will have them.

Although even sole proprietors need such a system, as an owner of a large horse-business operation, you will have addi-tional needs for an internal system of controls for your busi-ness. You will need to protect against errors, theft, and other losses. One means of accomplishing this is to divide the fi-nancial accounting and record-keeping tasks.

One partner, for example, might perform data entry for your horse business' various sources of income and expendi-tures, while another writes checks and reconciles the check-book. Or perhaps one of you writes the checks and the other reconciles the checkbook. If you sell supplies in your busi-ness, a third partner might periodically compare actual inven-tory to that listed on the books.

The more elaborate your business operation and the greater the number of owners or investors to whom you must report, the more important it will become to physically protect the data you generate about your business and to ensure that the data is error free. Of course, keeping the proper records also will be important. That is the subject of the next chapter.

GREEN FARM
Balance Sheet
As of December 31, 2000

ASSETS

Cash, cash equivalents $8,400.00

Equipment $89,000.00

Buildings $75,000.00

Farm land $300,000.00

Total Assets **$472,400.00**

LIABILITIES

Feed bill due now $3,400.00

Fertilizer, etc. due now $8,100.00

Equipment loan balance $17,000.00

Land, bldg. loan/note $54,000.00

Total Liabilities **$82,500.00**

EQUITY

Mr. Green's opening balance equity $370,857.00

Net ordinary income $19,043.00

Mr. Green's year-end equity (Net Worth) $389,900.00

Total Liabilities and Equity **$472,400.00**

GREEN FARM*
Profit and Loss

	Jan. 1, 2000 through Dec. 31, 2000	Jan. 1, 1999 through Dec. 31, 1999
ORDINARY INCOME		
General farm operations	$64,000.00	$70,000.00
Horse boarding	$16,000.00	$10,000.00
Trail use fees	$3,200.00	$0.00
Riding lessons	$4,400.00	$2,550.00
Total Income	**$87,600.00**	**$82,550.00**
ORDINARY EXPENSES		
Bank service charges	$57.00	$57.00
Legal fees	$1,500.00	$1,500.00
Supplies	$3,900.00	$6,330.00
Equipment purchase	$13,000.00	$7,000.00
Interest expense	$12,000.00	$4,800.00
Veterinarian fees	$6,000.00	$9,000.00
Payroll	$18,000.00	$16,000.00
Tax preparation fees	$300.00	$300.00
Misc.	$7,400.00	$11,250.00
Taxes	$6,400.00	$6,400.00
Total Expenses	**$68,557.00**	**$62,637.00**
Net Ordinary Income	**$19,043.00**	**$19,913.00**

*These numbers are not intended to resemble costs on an actual farm. They merely serve to show how such a document might look and the kinds of information one might gain from an examination of the documents from year to year. Check out the balance sheet to see where else the net ordinary income appears.

GREEN FARM
Cash Flow Projections/Assumptions

First Quarter 2001

	January	February	March
General farm operations	$1,000.00	$1,000.00	$1,500.00
Horse boarding	$1,200.00	$1,200.00	$1,200.00
Trail use fees	$100.00	$100.00	$300.00
Riding lessons	$200.00	$200.00	$400.00
Total Revenue	**$2,500.00**	**$2,500.00**	**$3,400.00**
Bank service charges	$0.00	$0.00	$28.00
Legal fees	$0.00	$0.00	$500.00
Supplies	$325.00	$400.00	$400.00
Equipment purchase	$1,083.00	$1,083.00	$1,083.00
Interest expense	$1,000.00	$1,000.00	$1,000.00
Veterinarian fees	$500.00	$1,000.00	$1,000.00
Payroll	$1,500.00	$1,500.00	$1,500.00
Tax preparation fees	$50.00	$0.00	$0.00
Misc.	$620.00	$620.00	$600.00
Taxes	$1,600.00	$0.00	$0.00
Total Expenses	**$6,678.00**	**$5,603.00**	**$6,111.00**

CHAPTER 2

Business Records You Should Keep

Two frequently asked questions from people starting new businesses are "what records should I keep?" and "for how long?" Neither of these questions has a simple answer, but in this chapter we will attempt to give you some general guidance. The length of time will vary somewhat depending upon the type of document and the purpose for which it is held.

As you operate your business, you will gain a sense of some of the records you will need for your particular horse business. Always err on the side of keeping more records than you think you actually need, but keep them organized. If you have lots of records that cannot be found when needed, it is much the same as not having the records at all.

RECORDS OF TRANSACTIONS

Records of transactions include some obvious business operations items such as bills and receipts for feed, veterinary care, utilities, etc. If you pay all bills by check, you will have an additional record of the transaction — the check itself. Paying by check gives you a measure of control, as well as knowledge of where your money goes. Cash tends to disappear quickly and is difficult to tie to any particular receipt or item of expense. At tax time, you must be able to document your expenditures to claim them as business deductions.

Open a separate bank account for your business, even if the business is very small. Many taxpayers get into difficulty by starting a small business using their family or personal checking account and then cannot satisfy the Internal Revenue Service that all expenses are business expenses if they are later audited. Never mix household and business purchases from the same account, even if it means separating items and writing two checks at the store.

AT A GLANCE

- Open a separate bank account for your business.

- Pay by check whenever possible.

- Each party to a contract should receive and maintain an original document.

- Keep property transfer records indefinitely.

- Some businesses need to register with the appropriate state or local agency.

Whenever possible, pay by check. Make full use of the memo section of each check that you write for your business. This will provide an extra source of information about the nature of the payment you made. Keep all canceled checks (or the duplicate copies, if your bank does not return checks), your bank statements, and check registers. Arrange them in numerical order.

Be sure to put complete beginning and ending dates on the fronts of check registers. If you later need to compare the register to a bank statement or check, it will be much easier if you can tell at a glance whether you should expect to find a particular check listed in a particular register. Keep these records for as long as necessary to ensure that they will not be subject to billing or payment disputes, contract claims, injury or damage claims, or tax audits.

The time factor for potential billing and payment disputes tends to be fairly short, as compared with the time you might have to keep records that could apply to contract claims, injury or damage claims, and tax audits. Each state has its own statutes of limitations for various types of legal claims that can be raised. These cannot be discussed in detail in this book.

As an example, however, in Kentucky a personal-injury claim can be brought to court for one year from the date a person knew or reasonably should have known of an injury. A contract claim can be brought for fifteen years. Your state will have its own rules about how long you or someone with whom you do business might be exposed to potential claims. Check with your attorney about the statute of limitations that may apply in your situation and in your state.

Each party to a contract should receive and maintain an original document. This requires you to execute at least two originals, as all contracts involve at least two parties. Never write or make notes on the original after it has been executed. If you have a need to make notations, make a photocopy first, and write only on the copy. Keep your copy for as long as any potential legal action could arise as a result of the contract.

Records pertaining to a transaction might also include a telephone log or even a diary or log of discussions. These can be helpful in the event a dispute over the terms of an agreement later arises. You should make it an ongoing part of your business procedures to write down at the time of the discussions or very shortly thereafter a summary of what you understood about a business agreement at the time.

It is not necessary to do this for every transaction or contract or agreement, but err on the side of caution for any large or expensive project, as well as any project that could end up in court if things go badly. While most people may be "good people" and most transactions have few real problems, you, as owner of your business, have a very real interest in protecting your business in those few situations where things don't go well. Unfortunately, you will not know until after the fact which situations will go awry.

Do not wait until after a dispute arises and then attempt

to reconstruct what was said or done. For one thing, memory fades over time. For another, if the dispute resulted in any sort of court action, you might be able to use, in support of your position, a log or diary that you routinely kept and in which you made contemporaneous, dated entries. If you simply write down your recollection long after a discussion actually occurred, you may be entirely prevented from using the document as evidence and will be less credible in any event.

RECORDS OF PROPERTY TRANSFERS

You should keep indefinitely records regarding transfer of any property by title or deed. If you own or purchase real estate as part of your horse business, you should keep a copy of the deed in a safe place. The same is true for automobiles, mobile homes, trailers, and anything for which you hold title. Keep with those documents any notes or mortgages or records of tax liens or judgment liens and releases of liens pertaining to the property you own.

Organize all documents in a manner that makes them easily identifiable in the event they are needed.

PAYROLL RECORDS

Keep all records regarding payroll. These include, among others, W-4s on which your employees indicate how many withholding allowances they intend to claim. You will then use this information throughout the year as you withhold taxes from their paychecks. You also should keep employer copies of the W-2s, on which income and withholding are reported to the Internal Revenue Service. You also may have substitute W-2s, such as 1099s, for independent contractors.

Other payroll records you should keep include I-9s (which are explained in a later chapter), wage and tax transmittal statements, state and local tax withholding records, unemployment insurance records, worker's compensation records, etc., for as long as you would keep tax records, unless your state requires a longer period. If you provide employee benefits, be sure to keep records of these. Check with your attorney about length of time to keep these records in your state.

Each employee should have a separate file in which his or her forms and records are kept. Make sure you know when to update such records. The Internal Revenue Service allows you to assume that information provided to you on a W-4 remains the same from year to year, unless an employee informs you otherwise. It is better practice to offer employees each year the opportunity to review their withholding allowances and make changes as appropriate.

Some of the payroll records, such as the wage and tax transmittal records, receipts for payments of taxes withheld, contributions to unemployment insurance, and so forth, do not relate to any one individual employee. Rather they summarize the payroll taxes paid by the business for all employees. Keep these separately, along with the other tax records of the business.

LEGAL DOCUMENTS THAT ESTABLISH YOUR BUSINESS

Even if you operate your business as a sole proprietor, you may have to register your business in your state and town or county. As a sole proprietor, you would not require a separate income tax identification number, but you might require a tax account number for sales or services provided to customers. Check with your attorney to find out the requirements for business registration if you are operating as a sole proprietor. Keep copies of any documents you are required to file in order to operate your business. If you subsequently decide to terminate the business, hold onto the records until, under your state's limitations periods, no one could have any claims against you because of the business.

A partnership is often required to file something in the

Secretary of State's Office that lists the name of the partnership, identifies at least one general partner, and lists the partnership's mailing address, as well as the address for service of process in case someone decides to file a lawsuit against the partnership. Generally, the service of process will be a street address because a complaint cannot be served to a post office box, even though such a box may be used for most business matters. You may have to file similar information in your county clerk's office.

Each business partner should receive and maintain an original copy of the partnership agreement. The partnership agreement specifies the name and terms of the business relationship, tells how the agreement can be changed, and the conditions under which the partnership will automatically terminate. The partnership agreement explains how partners will receive distributions and the responsibilities of the individual partners for liabilities of the business. In the event the partnership terminates, this document provides the mechanism for allocating assets and debts among the partners.

Corporations, once their existence is established by satisfying state registration requirements, are separate legal entities. In order to come into existence, each corporation will have to file, usually with the Secretary of State, an initial corporate charter, or articles of incorporation, and bylaws. Basically, the corporate charter or articles of incorporation identify the name of the business, the name of the person who is filing the papers (the legal mechanisms for this vary from state to state), the value of initial stock issued, and the business and street addresses of the business.

The bylaws identify the initial officers and directors and specify procedures for electing and/or appointing subsequent officers. Procedures for voting and establishing committees, duties of officers, and so on also will be found in the bylaws. An original of these documents should be kept with the person in the business charged with the responsibility for keeping the corporate records, along with any documentation that such documents have been properly filed.

Corporations are accountable to shareholders. The larger the number of shareholders, the more complex this can become. As a general matter, all minutes of stockholder and directors' meetings should be maintained in a separate minutes book and made available for inspection by the shareholders. This is more than good practice — it is often a legal requirement established by states. Check with your legal advisor to find out if your state has requirements as to the form of the information to be kept with the minutes book.

Many attorneys who practice in this area will not only help you establish the business, but also can help you obtain a corporate minutes book, stock certificates, and a corporate seal. All corporate records such as this must be maintained as long as the corporation exists or has any potential for liability to shareholders or any other person or entity. In addition to minutes books, corporations must maintain a record of all stock outstanding, including names and addresses of shareholders, numbers of shares held, classes of stock, and the values of each share.

ALL TAX RECORDS

A sole proprietor must keep, at a minimum, all personal income tax records for at least three years. Ten years is better practice. A sole proprietor who sells products also must develop and maintain records of any sales tax collected on behalf of the taxing authority.

A partnership, like a sole proprietor, pays no federal income tax at the entity level. Rather, the partnership obtains a federal tax identification number for use in reporting tax information on the partnership return and then files the informational return and gives to each partner a tax document showing his or her individual share of net ordinary income and certain other income and expenses that pass through to the individuals. Each general partner in a partnership should have received a copy of the income-tax informational forms filed on behalf of the partnership each year. For federal purposes, this is a Form 1065. Your state probably has a similar informational form. Local taxing authorities also may require informational reports.

This information from the informational return is then included in the partners' individual income tax return. Partnerships also report this information to their states. In some local taxing authorities, more than an informational return is required. Some Kentucky counties, for example, require payment of a tax on the net profits of the partnership prior to distribution to the individual partners. A local tax identification number is required for payment of these taxes. These records should be kept for at least as long as any tax records must be kept and perhaps longer for a long-term partnership.

A corporation is a separate entity and will be taxed as such. It must, therefore, have its own tax identification number at all levels of taxation. All tax records and tax identification numbers should be maintained in the same manner as other business entities keep such records.

INSURANCE POLICIES

It may sound obvious, but a surprising number of business people do not keep, in a way that anyone could find the information, copies of their insurance policies. At least one person other than yourself should know the location of all insurance policies and addenda. Keep the original policies and any changes of which the insurer informs you in a single location. This includes property insurance, life insurance, disability insurance, liability insurance, health insurance, and any other policy you may have that is in any way intended to protect your business from loss, to provide income or pay bills during periods of disability, or to provide for your family in the event something happens to you or the business. These should be kept for as long as the policy is in force or could be reinstated.

ESTATE PLANNING DOCUMENTS

A power of attorney lets someone else act for you when you are unavailable to act for yourself. The document that identifies the person or persons holding such powers should be maintained in a safe place and in a manner that makes it easily accessible to at least one other person. Suppose, for example, that you are a sole proprietor. For some reason you are unavailable or unable to sign an important document or pay a bill when it comes due. You have appointed someone to have power of attorney, but no one knows where the document is because you like to keep your privacy and don't want to risk that the person with authority to sign for you will take advantage of the power of attorney.

The person you have appointed cannot act without the piece of paper, properly executed (some localities also require this document to be filed in the county clerk's office or some other location), that says he or she can act for you. You may miss an opportunity that you wanted to take or fall into default on a loan simply because the person with power to act for you doesn't have access to the document giving him or her authority to act.

Your business also may be affected by the contents of your last will and testament or a trust agreement. These also should be maintained in a manner that is easily accessible to those who need them. Please remember that you can usually dispose of shares of stock in your corporate business and can pass on interests in a business (if your beneficiaries choose to continue to run the business) operated by you as a sole proprietorship through your will. If you have a partnership, however, it is the partnership agreement that will specify the terms for distribution of your partnership interest at your death. Often family members may not even know the form of ownership in which the business is held, making it critically important to keep all these records together.

CHAPTER 3

Taking the Work Out of Employer-Employee Relations

Unless your horse business truly falls into the "backyard" category, you probably have one or more employees to help you care for the animals and maintain the equipment and facilities. You may not feel like the "boss," especially if your business is small and you employ few people, but regardless of the size of your workforce, you have certain responsibilities and obligations toward those you employ. An exhaustive review of employment law and employer-employee relations is far beyond the scope of this book and for specific advice relating to your individual situation, you should consult your own attorney.

As an employer, you have a general duty to treat your employees fairly and to provide a safe workplace. Beyond that, there are certain principles that should guide your dealings with your workers.

EMPLOYMENT AT WILL

One of the initial decisions you must make when deciding to hire someone to work for you is whether to formalize the employment agreement in a written contract. We advocate written agreements whenever possible, not just in the employment context, but whenever possible in your business. Reducing a verbal agreement to writing forces the parties to be certain they both understand and agree on the important terms of the contract, and the written document can reduce misunderstandings if there is a dispute.

Despite a general consensus that written contracts are useful, there has been slow and reluctant acceptance of such formal agreements in the horse business. Horse dealings traditionally have been conducted on a handshake basis, and that trend continues today. The decision whether to use a written employment contract or to rely on a verbal agreement between you and your employees is a personal one, but it is a decision that should be made with the advice of legal counsel and with an understanding of the potential consequences.

AT A GLANCE

- No matter the size of your business, you have certain responsibilities and obligations toward those you employ.

- Written documents can reduce misunderstandings between employees and workers.

- All employers should be familiar with Title VII, which prohibits discrimination by an employer on the basis of race, color, religion, gender, or national origin.

No one hires an employee anticipating that the worker soon will create a problem and will have to be fired. Such situations develop with alarming frequency after the fact, however, and your ability to discharge an employee depends, in part, on whether there is a written employment contract. In Kentucky, and in most other states as well, a worker who is hired without a written employment contract for a specified term of employment is considered an employee "at will."

Status as an at-will employee traditionally meant that the worker could be fired at any time for any reason or without any reason at all. The employee literally worked at the will and whim of the employer. Clearly, this was not in the employee's best interest.

More recently, statutory protections against various forms of discrimination enacted at the federal and state level have limited somewhat the ability of an employer to discharge an at-will employee. An employer cannot fire an employee, even a worker without a written employment contract, based on the employee's race, national origin, gender, religion, or, in many instances, disability. Such groups are called "protected classes" and discrimination based on membership in such a class is prohibited.

Another recent trend is to provide some protection for at-will employees whose discharge violates a fundamental public policy. This can be difficult to define, but probably includes a firing because the employee exercised a statutory or constitutional right, refused to perform an illegal activity, or was a "whistle-blower" about an employer's illegal or improper practices. Beyond these restrictions, however, an at-will employee has few protections against discharge. Caution should be exercised, however, when discharging an at-will employee to avoid a wrongful discharge lawsuit.

An oral contract of employment for a specified period also can modify the at-will status of an employee, and a contract will be implied by a court in some circumstances based on the actions of the parties. The difficulty with such verbal and implied contracts is, first, proving their existence, and, second, establishing the relevant terms.

The situation becomes somewhat more complicated when there is a written employment contract. An employee serving under an employment contract for a specified period of time still can be discharged prior to the termination of the contract. The employer must establish negligence, lack of skill, gross inefficiency, dishonesty, or some other legitimate cause for the firing, or possibly face a lawsuit brought by the disgruntled ex-employee.

A contract employee also can be discharged if his or her position is eliminated due to legitimate economic business conditions. A downturn in the market for breeding seasons that encourages a farm to decide to stop standing stallions would be a legitimate reason to discharge the stallion manager, for example, even during the life of a valid employment contract. The principal restriction is that the economic condition cannot be a bad faith pretext for firing the employee.

The foregoing may sound like a good reason not to have a formal employment contract, because doing so restricts somewhat the freedom of an employer to discharge workers. Generally, though, the benefits of a written agreement with your employees far outweigh the problems that such an agreement causes, by setting out in detail the rights and obligations of each party. Your attorney can help draft an employment contract appropriate for your individual situation.

DISCRIMINATION IN THE WORKPLACE

Title VII of the Civil Rights Act of 1964 marked the first major attempt by Congress to prohibit discriminatory practices by private employers. In a nutshell, Title VII prohibits discrimination by an employer on the basis of race, color, religion, gender, or national origin. Discrimination on the basis of pregnancy and the problem of sexual harassment in the workplace are addressed under the general prohibition against discrimination based on gender. Sexual preference, however, is not covered by Title VII.

Since Title VII was enacted, Congress also has addressed other forms of employment discrimination and many states have passed similar legislation. State anti-discrimination laws may provide more protection than their federal counterparts, and if so, your business must comply with your individual state's requirements. Title VII, for example, applies to employers who are engaged in a business affecting interstate commerce, with 15 or more workers employed during a specified period of time. Kentucky's counterpart, KRS 344.100, on the other hand, defines a covered employer as a person or entity with eight or more employees during a specified period. Kentucky's law thus applies to many smaller businesses that would not fall under the umbrella of Title VII. Anti-discrimination laws in a majority of other states also apply to employers that are not covered under Title VII because of their number of employees.

Because the nature of state anti-discrimination laws and their application may vary somewhat from jurisdiction to jurisdiction, you should familiarize yourself both with federal requirements and with the law in your own area. Keep in mind, though, that an employer with only a few workers does not have free rein to discriminate, notwithstanding the statutory definition of "employer." The spirit, if not the letter, of this kind of legislation applies regardless of the size of your business, and impermissible discrimination in your business is fertile ground for a lawsuit under a variety of common-law legal theories.

The following brief summary of federal anti-discrimination laws is not intended to be exhaustive. Rather, it is intended to highlight some of the potential problem areas for an unwary employer and to encourage you to become familiar with federal laws that may affect the way you deal with your employees. Most states have similar legislation, and the application of both federal and state law to your horse business should be discussed with your attorney.

• Title VII of the Civil Rights Act of 1964 makes it unlawful for an employer to "fail or refuse to hire, discharge or otherwise discriminate against any individual with respect to compensation, terms, conditions or privileges of employment because of such individual's race, color, religion, sex or national origin." An employee who thinks that he or she has been discriminated against on the basis of one of the listed grounds has the option of either filing a charge with the Equal Employment Opportunity Commission or after receipt of a "right to sue" letter from the EEOC, bringing a lawsuit against the employer in state or federal court.

Remedies available to a successful civil litigant (the person initiating the lawsuit) include reinstatement to the position, back pay, and compensatory and punitive damages. (Unlike compensatory damages, punitive damages are designed to punish the wrongdoer.)

• The Age Discrimination in Employment Act of 1967

(ADEA) makes it unlawful for an employer to "fail or refuse to hire, discharge or otherwise discriminate against any individual with respect to his/her compensation, terms, conditions or privileges of employment because of such individual's age." The ADEA protects workers age 40 and older, and can be enforced by an employee in a manner similar to the enforcement procedures of Title VII. Remedies for a successful civil litigant can be substantial, including back pay, front pay, reinstatement, promotion, awards of seniority, and liquidated monetary damages.

• The Equal Pay Act of 1963 (EPA) makes it unlawful for an employer to discriminate on the basis of an employee's gender in the payment of wages for similar jobs. In other words, the EPA requires that an employer pay a comparable wage to male and female workers who are doing the same job under generally similar conditions, such as male and female exercise riders or grooms.

• The Americans with Disabilities Act of 1990 (ADA) prohibits discrimination by private employers against workers with disabilities. The ADA protections include prohibitions against discrimination based on disability in job application and interview procedures, hiring, promotion, wages, training, and most other terms and conditions of employment. The ADA includes a broad definition of disability to include persons with a physical or mental impairment that "substantially limits" one or more of the individual's major life activities; a person with a history of such impairment; or a person who is perceived as having such an impairment.

Major life activities include performing manual tasks, caring for oneself, walking, seeing, talking, hearing, breathing, and learning. Covered disabilities include physical and mental impairments, cosmetic disfigurement, learning disabilities, and infectious or communicable diseases (including HIV infection and AIDS). A history of alcoholism is a disability, as is prior drug use in a person who has completed a rehabilitation program; however, current use of illegal drugs is not considered a disability, nor is ongoing alcoholism that prevents an employee from doing his or her job in an efficient and safe manner.

The ADA prohibits pre-employment medical tests, but allows such tests during the period between an offer of employment and the time the worker starts on the job. Some employers require a pre-offer screening for illegal drugs, and there is dispute about whether this practice constitutes a prohibited "medical test." The ADA also prohibits an employer from asking a prospective employee if he or she has a disability, but allows questions about the person's ability to perform job-related tasks.

It is possible — and given the level of complexity of federal and state law — even probable that you can discriminate against a job applicant or an employee without intending to do so. Your current hiring practices, including questions you can and cannot ask job applicants, procedures for disciplining and discharging employees, wage plans, and all other facets of your scheme for employer-employee relations should be discussed with your attorney. In the area of employment, an ounce of prevention in the form of discussion and planning with your attorney truly is worth a pound of cure.

SEXUAL HARASSMENT

Sexual harassment, as noted earlier, is covered under Title VII and various state laws. The problem merits a separate section because it is so pervasive. Some reports suggest that as many as nine out of 10 female workers and two out of 10 male workers will experience some type of sexual harassment in the workplace during their employment.

The Equal Employment Opportunity Commission states:

Unwelcome sexual advances, requests for sexual favors, and other verbal or physical conduct of a sexual nature constitute sexual harassment when submission to or rejection of this conduct explicitly or implicitly affects an individual's employment, unreasonably interferes with an individual's work performance or creates an intimidating, hostile or offensive work environment.

This is a very broad definition of offensive conduct, one that includes both job-related demands for sexual favors (the legal term for this is quid pro quo sexual harassment) and the creation of a hostile work environment. In the former group of cases, the aggrieved worker only has to prove one instance of harassment; for the latter, a pattern of offensive conduct must be proved.

As an employer, you also may be liable if one of your employees is sexually harassed by a non-employee, such as a client or vendor who comes to the farm. You should establish a policy against sexual harassment (and other forms of discrimination, too), make your employees aware of the policy, and enforce it if there are violations. You also should establish and enforce a policy of confidentiality for employees who report incidents of alleged harassment. Having a stated and enforced policy against sexual discrimination will not protect you completely from a lawsuit, but failure to have such a policy may look incriminating to a jury. An attorney, preferably one familiar with employment law, can help you draft an effective policy that protects both you and your employees.

WORKER'S COMPENSATION

In Kentucky, as in most states, the worker's compensation program provides the exclusive remedy through which a covered employee who is injured on the job can recover from his or her employer. This means that an employee who is injured on the job and who receives money from a worker's compensation program cannot also sue his or her employer for damages.

Through participation in the program, an injured worker gives up the right to sue the employer — making worker's compensation payments to the employee the exclusive remedy for injury — while gaining the right to recover through the system without having to show fault on the part of the employer for an injury.

The mechanics and application of worker's compensation programs vary from state to state. Generally, the programs require a covered employer to obtain insurance to cover his or her employees in the event of injury or occupational disease, with the premiums varying based on the number of workers and other factors. By doing so, the employer obtains a statutory defense to a lawsuit brought by an injured employee.

Whether you will be required to participate is a matter of state law. In Kentucky, for example, although most workers are included in the worker's compensation program by statutory mandate, those employed in agricultural businesses are not. A variety of state court decisions have determined that the agricultural exemption in the worker's compensation program includes businesses that condition and exercise racehorses that have been at the track but have been returned to a farm for rehabilitation due to injury. Businesses that board and breed horses also are exempt. So, depending on the nature of your business and where it is located, you may or may not be required to participate as an employer in the state's program.

Even if you are not required to participate in your state's worker's compensation program, most jurisdictions — including Kentucky — allow employers not otherwise covered to participate voluntarily. The owner of a Kentucky Thoroughbred breeding farm with several employees may, for example, purchase the required insurance and elect to join the state's worker's compensation program voluntarily. By so doing, the employer has insulated himself from lawsuits by injured employees, while at the same time creating an attractive enticement for prospective workers.

Whether you are required to participate in your state's

worker's compensation program, and, if not, whether you should voluntarily participate, are questions for your attorney.

MINIMUM WAGE

With passage of the Fair Labor Standards Act of 1938, a minimum wage of $.25/hour was established. At this writing, the minimum wage is $5.15/hour for non-supervisory, non-farm, private sector employees, with some support in Congress for an increase above that figure in the near future. The minimum wage for workers in agriculture is less, based on statute.

Most states, including Kentucky, adopt the federal minimum-wage standards by reference. Some states have minimum-wage standards set higher than the federal minimum, a few have a lower minimum wage than the federal standard (in which case the higher federal minimum applies), and a very few states have no minimum wage at all (the federal standards apply here as well).

You should be able to determine the minimum wage for farm workers in your state with a telephone call to your state wage and hour department or to the U.S. Department of Labor's Wage and Hour Division. As always, if there are questions, you should consult an attorney in your state to determine the minimum wage for your particular business. Your attorney also can tell you whether you are required to post an informational poster for employees that outlines employer-employee rights and obligations for your workers.

Finally, keep in mind that a minimum wage establishes a floor, not a ceiling, for what you pay your employees and that a legally mandated minimum wage is not necessarily a living wage.

SAFETY IN THE WORKPLACE

The Occupational Health and Safety Act (OSHA) of 1970 represented an attempt by Congress to provide comprehensive regulation of health and safety issues in the workplace. The law imposes a general requirement on virtually every private employer — including you — to provide a workplace free of dangerous tasks and conditions. Many states have adopted their own occupational health and safety programs, which, if approved by the federal government, assume front-line responsibility for enforcement of workplace safety standards.

Kentucky's Occupational Health and Safety and Health Program received final federal approval in 1985. It mirrors federal legislation in most respects and is typical of many similar state plans.

Kentucky law imposes on every employer both a general and specific duty. First, each employer "shall furnish to each of his employees employment and a place of employment which are free from recognized hazards that are causing or are likely to cause death or serious physical harm to his employees." Second, each employer must comply with any standards relevant to his or her particular business issued under the state program. State law imposes a duty on each employee to comply with occupational health and safety standards and applicable rules and regulations.

Kentucky's law also requires every employer to keep records of occupational injuries and illnesses, post a summary of those statistics for the information of employees, and maintain the records for five years. Finally, an employer cannot discriminate against an employee who reports a possible violation to authorities or who requests an inspection of the place of employment.

There appear to be few specific safety standards or regulations directly applicable to horse farms, although some of the general agricultural standards might be applicable, depending on the actual nature of your business. The possibilities for violations of the general obligation to provide a safe workplace on a horse farm are virtually endless, however. Problems could result from poorly maintained or dangerous farm equipment, for example, or from improper storage of fertilizers, insecticides, and other commonly used chemicals, hazardous conditions in a hayloft, or possibly even keeping an unmanageable stallion.

Penalties for violations can be severe. For a willful or repeated violation, for example, a civil penalty of $5,000 to $70,000 may be assessed if the violation is determined to be serious; a maximum penalty of $7,000 may be assessed for a violation determined not to be of a serious nature.

The world of employer-employee relations is a complex one, with myriad opportunities for problems. The value of a written contract should be obvious in this context; by allowing both parties to begin the employment relationship with a clear understanding of what each expects, the chances for misunderstandings are substantially reduced.

THE IMMIGRATION AND NATURALIZATION SERVICE

Anyone who doubts that the employment of foreign nationals has become essential to the success — and sometimes the survival — of the horse business need only stroll though the backstretch of a racetrack or the stable area of a horse show, or visit any one of the majority of horse operations in the country. Foreign nationals play a vital role, but with their growing numbers in the workplace have come increased demands on employers.

A foreign national without a green card or government authorization to work in one of a number of specified employment categories who finds a job in the United States can be deported by the government if discovered. Until the mid-1980s, however, the employer of an undocumented alien faced neither criminal nor civil liability for having hired a foreign national who did not have employment permission from the INS. Employers traditionally could hire illegal aliens without fear of repercussion.

That situation changed with passage of the Immigration Reform and Control Act of 1986 and the Immigration Act of

1990. The former, particularly, fundamentally changed the way employers must deal with foreign nationals by shifting the enforcement burden for policing the country's immigration laws to private employers. The full impact of this legislation is far beyond the scope of this book. Questions about the various alternatives open to an employer who intends to bring foreign nationals to the United States for either permanent or temporary work, including an explanation of the different visa categories, should be directed to an immigration attorney.

Employers now must verify both the authority to work and the identity of each person hired, either before a final job offer is made (the preferable option) or within three days after employment starts. This verification is made through completion by both the employer and employee of INS Form I-9. The employee must provide either a single document that establishes both identity and authorization to work or separate documents. Originals must be provided.

Documents that establish both identity and authorization to work include a U.S. passport (either current or expired), a Certificate of U.S. Citizenship, a Certificate of Naturalization, or an unexpired Temporary Resident or Employment Authorization Card. Documents that establish identity alone include a driver's license with photograph or identifying data, a government identification card, a school identification card with photograph, or voter registration card. Documents that establish eligibility to work include a U.S. social security card or an original or certified copy of a birth certificate issued by a state, county, or municipal authority in this country. (This list is not inclusive, and you should contact the INS for a complete listing of acceptable documents.)

The employer must state under oath and penalty of perjury that he or she has examined the offered documents, that the documents appear on their face to be genuine, and that the person presenting them is eligible to work in the United States. Employers cannot request "more or different" documents than are required nor can they refuse to honor documents that appear to be genuine. Good-faith compliance with the verification requirements by the employer is a defense to a violation.

Finally, it is important to keep in mind that the INS verification procedures are required for all employees, not just employees who obviously are foreign nationals.

THE EMPLOYEE HANDBOOK

As an employer, you generally are not required to distribute to your workers an employee handbook. If you decide to do so, you should be aware that courts may interpret your statements in the manual as creating an employment contract, even if that was not your intention.

That potential problem aside, the advantages of an employee handbook probably outweigh the disadvantages, by reducing the risk of misunderstandings between you and your workers. The employee manual should include all relevant conditions of employment, such as expected work hours, duties, policies about overtime and sick pay, health and worker's compensation insurance benefits, any other benefits, and circumstances that can be expected to lead to dismissal.

The employee handbook also should make it clear that you have a zero-tolerance policy for violence, discrimination, and sexual harassment, and you should state the policy on firearms on the job. If you employ foreign nationals, you should provide any written material in a language that can be understood by your employees. Finally, you should require your employees to indicate in writing that they have received a copy of the handbook, and that notice of receipt should be kept in the worker's personnel file.

VIOLENCE IN THE WORKPLACE

Protestations of mail carriers aside, the phrase "going postal" has entered our vocabulary as shorthand for an employee who goes berserk and injures or kills fellow employees or others. Keeping in mind that anti-discrimination legislation limits somewhat the types of questions you can ask of a potential employee in a pre-employment interview, there still are things you can do to protect yourself and your business from potentially violent employees.

Experts agree that one of the best predictors of future violent behavior is a history of violence. In your interview you can, and should, ask a person about prior criminal convictions. If the job prospect has a history of violent crimes, that could be a valid ground for your refusing to make an offer of employment. You also should consider having an investigation firm conduct a criminal background check on your prospective employee.

The job application process should include a request for information about past employment, and then you should attempt to verify that the information provided is correct. Although many former employers are reluctant to discuss anything beyond dates of employment, out of fear of a defamation lawsuit if negative information is conveyed, you should make the effort.

As noted elsewhere, the ADA limits the types of questions that you can ask during a pre-offer job interview. The ADA also may limit your ability to require a pre-offer drug screen because such tests generally are regarded as medical tests, prohibited at that stage of the hiring process. Medical tests, including drug screens, are allowed during the period between the time when a job offer is made and when the employee actually starts work. Once the person is offered a job, you legally can make employment contingent on the employee passing a drug test. If the person fails, the job offer can be withdrawn at that point without liability on the part of the employer. It is important to require all employees for similar positions to take the same test to avoid charges of discrimination.

Although helpful, pre-offer investigation and pre-employment drug tests will not disclose all potentially violent employees. The best time to spot violent tendencies is after the employee starts working, and you should establish — and strictly enforce — a policy of zero tolerance for violence at your place of business. This provision can be included in an employment contract and in your employee handbook, and you also should emphasize during the hiring process that any violent behavior toward other employees, clients, or animals will result in immediate dismissal.

It always is better to be safe than sorry when the issue is violence in the workplace.

CHAPTER 4

Buying and Selling

Just as you must determine the form of ownership for your horse business, you also must decide the nature of the business. If you choose to board or train horses for others, you can expect a fairly regular flow of income, assuming that you have clients and that they pay their bills on time. If you have a breeding operation or competition stable, on the other hand, your primary sources of income will come from sales of your horses, and your cash flow likely will be anything but steady.

Your sales options primarily are public auction or private sale. The former typically are structured affairs, with the rights and obligations of the seller and buyer laid out in great detail in the sales company's Conditions of Sale. More common are private sales, which are the focus of this chapter.

The Uniform Commercial Code (UCC) is a body of law that governs a wide variety of commercial transactions, including the sale of goods. Some version of the UCC has been adopted by all 50 states, and although you may be unfamiliar with it now, you should be aware that the UCC comes into play every time you sell or buy a horse. (Horses, foals *in utero*, and most shares in stallions and other horses fall under the UCC definition of "goods.")

As a seller, you want to encourage a potential client to buy your horse, but you generally do not want to make specific promises about the horse's ability or guarantees about future success in the show ring, on the racetrack, or even as a pleasure horse. The buyer, on the other hand, has specific ideas about what he or she wants in a horse and may expect assurances from the seller that the horse fits the bill.

> ## AT A GLANCE
>
> • The Uniform Commercial Code governs the sale of goods, including horses.
>
> • The law may impose some implied warranties in a horse transaction.
>
> • The buyer and seller should execute a bill of sale any time a horse is sold.

Neither approach is totally realistic, and Article 2 of the UCC attempts to set a middle ground between the concerns of the seller and the desires of the buyer when it comes to warranties. Usually associated with automobiles and large appliances, a warranty is simply a promise that the article being sold will perform in a certain way. Warranties can be either express or implied, depending on the circumstances surrounding the sale.

As a seller, you create an express warranty anytime you make a positive statement of fact about a horse or when you describe the horse, so long as the buyer relies on the statement of fact or the description when deciding to buy the horse. This is true even if you do not intend to make a warranty. Advertising a show horse as a pony, which under American Horse Shows Association Rules means 14 hands, two inches or less in height, creates an express warranty about the height of your horse.

Some statements, called "puffery," are just what the name implies and do not form the basis of an express warranty, even though they are positive statements about a horse. Telling a potential buyer that the horse under consideration is the fastest or prettiest or smartest horse on the planet are examples of puffing, statements that no reasonable buyer would accept as true.

In addition to any express warranties you might make, either on purpose or inadvertently, the law may impose certain implied warranties on the horse you are selling. One is the warranty of title, which means that when you offer a horse for sale, you are promising that you have a good and marketable title to the animal, and that there are no liens or other security interests about which the buyer is unaware. In other words, when you offer a horse for sale, the buyer is entitled to believe that you have the right to sell the animal and to transfer full title.

A second type of implied warranty is the warranty of merchantability, which applies to sellers who hold themselves out as having some particular knowledge or expertise about horses. If the seller is a "merchant" under the UCC, the horse being sold must satisfy the contract description and be suitable to the general purposes for which it is being sold.

A third kind of implied warranty, the warranty of fitness for a particular purpose, may arise if before the sale is complete, the seller becomes aware of any particular purpose the buyer has in mind for the horse and learns that the buyer is relying on the seller to provide such an animal. In this situation, the buyer is entitled to rely on the seller's implied promise that the horse will suit the intended purpose.

This kind of transaction is common in the horse business. A buyer comes to you and says he is looking for a dressage horse capable of winning at third- and fourth-level competitions. Your knowledge that the buyer is looking for a particular kind of horse, and that he is relying on your expertise and advice, means that the horse you sell probably comes with an implied warranty that the animal is ready to at least compete at third and fourth level.

A seller can under some circumstances disclaim the implied warranties of merchantability and fitness for a particular purpose. Such disclaimers should be, and in the case of a disclaimer of fitness for a particular purpose, must be in writing. A seller also can disclaim warranties by selling the horse "as is" or "with all faults," although the market for such a horse may be extremely limited.

A seller also can request that a buyer examine the horse completely before finalizing the sale. If the buyer either has the horse examined or declines to do so, there no longer are any implied warranties covering conditions that could have been discovered during the examination.

If the buyer discovers a problem after completing the sale but before "accepting" the horse, the animal can be rejected and returned to the seller. Under the UCC, a buyer still can reject the horse within a reasonable time after taking physical possession of the animal. In other words, acceptance of the horse and taking physical possession are not the same under the UCC. If the problem goes undiscovered for a significant period of time, however, the UCC does not authorize returning the animal to the seller. Instead, the buyer must file a lawsuit for damages based on the seller's breach of either an express or implied warranty. At this point, the parties might consider some form of non-judicial alternative dispute resolution, which is discussed in a later chapter.

THE BILL OF SALE

The seller and buyer should execute a written bill of sale every time a horse is sold. There is no standard form for a bill of sale, but, at a minimum, your sale agreements should include:

1. Identity of the parties and description of the horse.

2. Demand from the seller that a complete and thorough inspection of the horse be made and acknowledgment by the buyer that an opportunity for such inspection was offered.

3. Language similar to the following, in conspicuous type and location:

SELLER MAKES NO WARRANTIES OR REPRESENTATIONS WHATSOEVER, EXPRESS OR IMPLIED, WITH RESPECT TO THE HORSE, INCLUDING WARRANTIES CONCERNING THE

PHYSICAL CONDITION, HEALTH, OR SOUNDNESS OF THE HORSE, OR WARRANTIES OR REPRESENTATIONS WITH RESPECT TO THE MERCHANTABILITY OR FITNESS OF THE HORSE FOR ANY PARTICULAR PURPOSE, ALL OF WHICH WARRANTIES ARE HEREBY EXCLUDED. THE PARTIES TO THIS AGREEMENT ACKNOWLEDGE THAT THE HORSE IS SOLD "AS IS" AND "WITH ALL FAULTS." BUYER ACKNOWL-EDGES THAT HE HAS CONDUCTED SUCH INVESTIGA-TIONS AND INSPECTIONS, INCLUDING THE USE OF A QUALIFIED VETERINARIAN, AND IS SATISFIED WITH THE HORSE'S CONDITION.

4. The purchase price, and, if relevant, provision for install-ment payments. If there are to be installment payments, the seller and buyer also should execute a separate promissory note for the unpaid portion of the purchase price.

5. Warranty by the seller of good and marketable title.

6. If there are installment payments, the definition of events that will constitute a default on the part of the buyer, and the seller's remedies in the event of a default.

7. A statement setting a date on which the risk of loss passes from the seller to the buyer.

8. A statement outlining when and where the horse will be delivered by the seller to the buyer.

9. The date upon which the buyer becomes responsible for boarding charges if the buyer does not take immediate deliv-ery of the horse.

10. An agreement between the parties as to the governing law and where any disputes will be litigated if non-judicial resolution is not possible.

11. Prohibition against assignment by the buyer of any in-terest in the sale agreement without consent of the seller.

12. Signatures of the parties and the effective date of the agreement.

The majority of horse sales, just like most other transac-tions in the horse business, proceed from inception to con-clusion without problems. As a result, it is easy to assume

that there will not be problems in any of your business dealings. This is not a realistic way to do business, however.
Instead, hope for the best, but prepare for the worst. Plan
your business transactions with an eye toward preventing
problems by making sure that the parties to a sale understand their rights and obligations before money changes
hands.

CHAPTER 5

The Taxman Cometh

Dear Taxpayer:
Welcome to your simplified tax return.

Line 1—How much money did you make last year?
$_____
Line 2—Send it in.

Thank you.
The Internal Revenue Service

Paying your taxes never has been and probably never will be as simple as this old joke suggests. The taxman does seem to be an unwelcome and consistently greedy partner in your business, though, considering the myriad of federal and state income taxes, sales and use taxes, employment taxes, social security withholding, and local license fees that must be paid. You cannot even escape by dying, as anyone who has been forced to deal with estate taxes can attest.

Although paying taxes never will be a painless experience, it can be a predictable one. Perhaps the only thing worse than having to pay taxes at all is finding that the tax bill is larger than you expected. While every reader's tax situation is different, there are some general problems and concerns faced by nearly everyone in the horse business, and we hope the following pages give you something to discuss with your tax adviser before the return is due.

THE HOBBY HORSE DILEMMA

For some people, owning horses is a pleasurable hobby with no expectation of profit. Many others run profit-motivated horse businesses, but often the expectation of profit exceeds the realization at the end of the tax year. Ideally, such horse-business losses can be deducted against income

> # AT A GLANCE
>
> • Your horse business has to meet certain criteria before you can deduct losses.
>
> • IRS regulations spell out nine factors that must be considered when deciding whether your horse operation qualifies as a for-profit business.
>
> • To "materially participate" in your horse business, you must spend 500 hours per tax year involved in the activity.

from other sources, reducing the horse owner's overall tax burden, but in reality this often is not the case.

Wary of people who might characterize their expensive recreational horse activities as businesses in an attempt to gain a tax advantage, the Internal Revenue Service in 1969 enacted Section 183 of the tax code. Better known as the "hobby loss provision," Section 183 has confounded horse people for more than a quarter-century. Simple in theory but difficult in practice, Section 183 says that losses from any activity (not just horse activities) can be used to reduce income from other profitable business ventures only if the activity generating the losses is "engaged in for profit."

Consider, for example, a taxpayer who owns two businesses: a restaurant that last year turned a $100,000 profit and a small stable of show horses that during the same period generated losses of $25,000. According to Section 183, the taxpayer can use the $25,000 loss from the show stable to reduce the $100,000 profit from the restaurant business for income tax purposes only if the taxpayer's horse activity was engaged in for profit.

Clearly, it is to the taxpayer's advantage to have his show

stable be considered an activity "engaged in for profit" because such a determination will result in a lower tax bill for the year. If, on the other hand, a determination is made that the show stable is not an activity "engaged in for profit," the taxpayer will not be able to deduct the stable's losses against his restaurant business income.

But how does your horse activity qualify? The easiest and most certain way is to show a profit, at least occasionally. Section 183 provides that any activity with a major emphasis on breeding, training, showing, or racing horses will be presumed to be an activity engaged in for profit if the activity shows a profit for two of the seven consecutive taxable years ending with the year under consideration. (This provision represents one of the few positive things in the current tax code for horse enthusiasts. Non-horse activities must show a profit in three of five years.)

For an ongoing activity, the "profit presumption" applies to the second year in which there is a profit, with the seven-year "safe" period starting with the first profitable year.

An established show stable with the following balance sheet thus will be presumed to satisfy the requirements of Section 183, unless the IRS can prove to the contrary, for the seven-year period running from 1995 through 2001:

2000	loss
1999	profit
1998	loss
1997	loss
1996	loss
1995	profit
1994	loss

A taxpayer has some discretion about when the IRS determination regarding the nature of the activity is made. When a taxpayer should make such an election and the varied factors that should be considered are well beyond the scope of this chapter. Specific questions should be addressed to your tax adviser.

Despite satisfying the Section 183 presumption, two profitable years out of seven do not guarantee that the IRS will not attempt to show that your horse activity has no profit motive, especially if two years of negligible profits are balanced against five years of very large losses. On the other hand, there is not a negative presumption — that the activity is not engaged in for profit — against a taxpayer who does not show a profit in at least two of seven years. In that situation, the taxpayer must rely on several factors to establish that the horse activity satisfies Section 183.

THE QUACK TEST

An old saying holds that if something looks like a duck, walks like a duck, and quacks like a duck, it probably is a duck. The IRS uses a similar test to determine whether a horse activity satisfies the Section 183 threshold when the two-profitable-years-out-of-seven presumption cannot be met. If your horse activity is conducted in a businesslike manner, it will be easier to convince the IRS of your profit motive.

IRS regulations spell out nine factors that must be considered when making the business/hobby determination. The regulations specify that no single factor is determinative, and that all facts and circumstances of the individual activity must be taken into account.

The nine factors are:

1. The manner in which the taxpayer carries on the activity. Conducting your activity in a business-like way, with complete and accurate books and records and separate business accounts, can indicate a profit motive. At a bare minimum, you should maintain separate financial and business records and checking accounts and employ a professional accountant with experience in the horse business, if possible. The IRS also may compare your operating methods with those of other similar businesses that are profitable.

2. The expertise of the taxpayer or his advisers. Although it should go without saying, you either need to become an expert in your horse activity or employ someone else who is. It will be very difficult to convince the IRS that you expect to show a profit with your sport horse breeding operation if you have not done your homework or if you do not hire someone who is an expert in the sport horse business. You will face a similar problem if you have the necessary expertise or hire someone who gives you good advice then fail to conduct the activity in a way you or your advisers recognize is likely to be profitable.

3. The time and effort expended by the taxpayer in carrying on the activity. The IRS expects you either to devote a substantial amount of time to your horse activity or to hire knowledgeable and competent persons to do the work for you. If you fail to do either, proving a profit motive to the IRS will be difficult.

4. Expectation that assets used in the activity may appreciate in value. Purchasing land that you expect to appreciate in value for your horse activity may indicate an expectation of profit, but there are specific IRS regulations that may limit the applicability of this approach. You may also be able to point to the appreciation in value of a horse — a successful racehorse or show horse that is being syndicated, for example — as an indicator of your profit motive.

5. The success of the taxpayer in carrying on other similar or dissimilar activities. A proven track record in other horse pursuits may help you convince the IRS that your current activity has a profit motive, even if it is unprofitable at the present time.

6. The taxpayer's history of income or losses with respect to the activity. The IRS notes, helpfully, that if you show a profit in a "series of years," it is a good indication that you have a profit motive for your horse activity.

7. The amount of occasional profits, if any, that are earned. In general, a substantial profit every now and then is better than a series of modest profits, especially if the occasional profits are small in comparison to the losses or to your investment in the activity. The obvious way to generate profits for a horse activity is through sales of horses, and it may be advantageous to concentrate your sales in one tax year as much as possible. Again, though, your tax professional should be consulted to help plan a comprehensive sales strategy.

8. The financial status of the taxpayer. The IRS is more likely to attribute a profit motive to a horse activity that is the taxpayer's sole source of income. On the other hand, a taxpayer with a losing horse activity and several other profitable businesses will have a harder sell, especially if, as the IRS puts it, "there are personal or recreational elements involved."

9. Elements of personal pleasure or recreation. This factor may be the most troublesome because it seems to suggest that there cannot be a profit motive in an activity you also happen to enjoy. This makes sense from the IRS perspective, because a "hobby loss" is precisely what Section 183 is supposed to curtail. On the other hand, the mere fact that you enjoy your horse activity does not automatically mean that there is no profit motive.

Application of IRS rules and regulations confounds tax experts and novices alike. The best way to understand Section 183 and the "hobby loss" regulations is to see them in action in the following examples. Both are actual cases decided by the U.S. Tax Court in September 2000.

WINNERS...

The taxpayers in the first example began breeding, showing, and selling Quarter Horses in 1993, and they expanded to open a boarding operation in 1995. They also leased some of their horses. From 1993 through 1996, their horse business produced gross income of $16,296 and generated total losses during the same period of $89,678. The taxpayers used the losses to reduce their taxable income from other sources. After an initial determination that the activity was not operated for profit, the IRS assessed additional taxes of $13,398 for 1995 and $10,687 for 1996. The taxpayers appealed to the U.S.Tax Court.

Because the horse activity did not ever show a profit, the two-of-seven presumption did not apply. Instead, the Tax Court applied the nine factors mentioned earlier in this chapter as follows:

1) The court found that the taxpayers conducted their business in a "serious and organized manner." The court noted that the taxpayers had lifelong experience with horses and that they used that expertise in the establishment and operation of the business. The taxpayers kept accurate records of both the activity's finances and the records of their horses, continually expanded and improved the facilities at their farm, and expanded into boarding and leasing their horses to others while starting to acquire quality broodmares.

The taxpayers did much of the work on the farm themselves to help reduce expenses. The taxpayers did not have a separate business checking account during their first years of operation, but the court said that their computerized records allowed them to generate reports of horse-related income and expenses. The court also noted that the taxpayers consulted experts, including an accountant to help set up their bookkeeping system and an attorney to draft boarding and leasing contracts. The first factor favored the taxpayers.

2) Citing the experience of the taxpayers, the court also noted that they "read books and periodicals, viewed videotapes, attended seminars, and consulted with experts." The court determined that the taxpayers had sufficient expertise to conduct a profitable business. The second factor favored the taxpayers.

3) The court found that the taxpayers devoted a significant amount of time to their horse business. The third factor favored the taxpayers.

Whether you want to have fun at the races (1), compete in Western or English events (2, 3), or keep breeding stock (4), you must strike a balance between the fun aspects and the business side of horse ownership.

If your goal is to make a profit, be sure to conduct your horse operation in a businesslike manner. This can include making capital improvements to your property, going to sales to upgrade your stock, and syndicating a racehorse or show horse to appreciate its value.

If you have employees, it is up to you to provide a safe and fair working environment, whether on the farm or at a racetrack or show stable.

Working with horses is inherently risky. As an employer, you must determine whether you are required or should volunteer to participate in worker's compensation programs in your state.

Conditions of Sale at public auctions (1) set out the rights of the buyer and seller. However, sellers are not required to announce all medical conditions, so the prudent buyer still does his or her homework (2).

In private sales (3), certain implied warranties, such as fitness and marketability, are imposed by law.

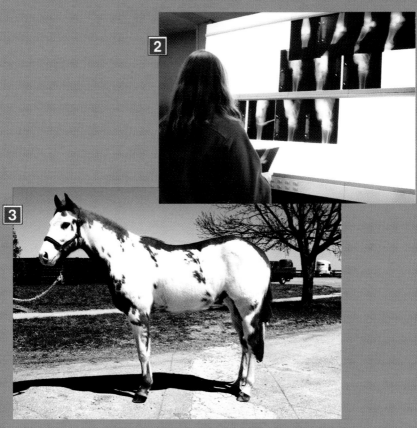

You could need additional liability insurance if you maintain a riding stable (1) or trail riding business (3) as opposed to strictly a boarding operation (2).

Disasters such as freak paddock accidents and barn fires can strike at any time. Equine mortality insurance can help an owner recoup at least a partial investment when a horse dies.

If you choose to do your own research, the Internet has many resources, but it is still best to consult with your team of advisers — which should include a veterinarian, attorney, and accountant — before making decisions that will affect your horse business.

4) Although the taxpayers testified that they expected the value of their horses to appreciate enough to cover the business losses, the court found the evidence to be inconclusive. The fourth factor favored neither the taxpayers nor the IRS.

5) The court noted that although the taxpayers had been successful in other business ventures, none was sufficiently similar to their horse activity to enable the Court to reach a conclusion. The fifth factor favored neither the taxpayers nor the IRS.

6) Because the taxpayers' business was relatively young, the court was unable to reach any conclusions regarding their history of income or loss. The sixth factor favored neither the taxpayers nor the IRS.

7) Although the taxpayers' business had not shown a profit, the court found this to be reasonable during the start-up years of the activity. The court also took note of the fact that one of the taxpayers' broodmares and her foal had died in 1994, reducing by one-fourth the taxpayers' broodmare band. The seventh factor favored neither the taxpayers nor the IRS.

8) The IRS argued that the taxpayers' substantial non-farm income indicated that they did not have a profit motive for their horse activity. The court did not agree, noting an almost 40 percent drop in the taxpayers' non-farm income from 1995 to 1996 and the facts that one of the taxpayers retired in 1993 and that another expected to retire in 1998 as indicating no long-term need to shelter income. The eighth factor favored neither the taxpayers nor the IRS.

9) The court found that although the taxpayers enjoyed breeding and showing their horses, their decisions to board and lease horses were not motivated by personal pleasure. The ninth factor favored neither the taxpayers nor the IRS.

With three of the nine factors favoring the taxpayers and the other six favoring neither the taxpayers nor the IRS, the court ruled that there was a legitimate profit motive during the years in question.

The taxpayers in this example did some things wrong, such

as mingling their personal and business funds in the same checking account, but they did many more things right. They evaluated the market and predicted a growing interest in Quarter Horses in their area; they maintained complete and accurate business records; they worked to keep expenses low; they changed their business plan in logical ways in attempts to make money; they studied to expand their own expertise and also sought and relied upon the advice of knowledgeable persons in the Quarter Horse business; and they retained experts, such as an accountant and an attorney, for assistance.

By operating their Quarter Horse operation like a business, the taxpayers were successful in countering IRS arguments that the activity was merely a hobby.

...AND LOSERS

The taxpayers in this example were husband and wife, both of whom had full-time, non-farm employment. The wife had been involved with horses her entire life and had a degree in microbiology with an emphasis in pre-med for veterinarians.

They started breeding Paso Finos in 1987. Although they had general knowledge and experience with horses, they had no specialized knowledge about Paso Finos. They never took any classes or attended seminars regarding either the financial or business aspects of raising horses. Also, unlike the taxpayers in the first example, this couple did not do any research into the marketability of Paso Finos, nor did they have any sort of business plan to guide them. They also did not seek any expert assistance before buying their first Paso Finos. Instead, the taxpayers chose Paso Finos because they liked the horses' appearance and smooth gait and because they thought the horses would be good for people with back problems.

The taxpayers did secure the assistance of a bloodstock agent, but his advice was questionable. For example, while encouraging veterinary pre-purchase examinations for horses that he recommended the taxpayers buy from others, he discouraged such examinations for horses he sold them. The taxpayers did not sell any horses for seven years, then when they did start selling horses, the sales frequently were to cull less-desirable animals. Generally poor record-keeping made it impossible to allocate expenses to each horse sold, and impossible to determine whether some — or any — of the sales were profitable.

The taxpayers kept their horses on a "modest and functional" California farm, where they did much of the maintenance and improvements. The Court noted that although the taxpayers kept voluminous records, the record-keeping activities were aimed at recording deductible expenses and were not directed toward generating financial reports that could have been used to track the success, or lack thereof, of the activity or to predict future profitability.

Finally, the taxpayers also had operated two other businesses, a dog-breeding operation and an antiques store, neither of which were generally profitable.

From 1987 through 1997, the taxpayers' Paso Fino operation never approached profitability. For those years, a total loss of $542,751 was reported. Following an audit for the years 1991, 1992, and 1993, the IRS made an initial determination that the taxpayers' were not operating their Paso Fino farm for profit.

Because there were no profitable years, the taxpayers were not entitled to rely on the presumption of a profit motive discussed earlier. The Tax Court relied, instead, on an evaluation of the nine relevant factors.

1) The court determined that the taxpayers' record-keeping system was insufficient because no evidence was presented to show that the records "were used to implement cost-saving measures or to improve profitability" and that the taxpayers did not "prepare any financial statements, profit and loss projections, budgets, breakdown analyses, or marketing

surveys." While giving the taxpayers credit with attempting to breed their mares every year, sometimes to well-bred, established stallions, the court characterized their marketing efforts as "unfocused and anemic." The court also noted that despite a lack of success selling their horses, the taxpayers never changed their marketing strategy.

Finding the "trappings of a business" to be absent, the court concluded that the taxpayers did not operate their farm in a businesslike fashion. The first factor favored the IRS.

2) Although the taxpayers did consult with other breeders from time to time, there was no indication that they had sought the advice of anyone before deciding to raise Paso Fino horses. The court found that the taxpayers "did not prepare for the economic aspects of the activity by study or consultation with experts" and that before starting their business they had no "concept of what their ultimate costs might be, how they might achieve any degree of cost efficiency, the amount of revenue they could expect, or what risks might impair the production of such revenue." The second factor favored the IRS.

3) Despite holding down full-time jobs, the taxpayers also managed their Paso Fino farm during the years at issue. They hired someone to clean stalls, but they did the rest of the work themselves, including feeding, grooming, training, bookkeeping, and paying bills. The court explained that while it was "clear the taxpayers loved their horses and enjoyed some of the farm work, there were many tasks, such as feeding, washing, and worming the animals," that had no recreational value. The third factor favored the taxpayers.

4) The court determined that the taxpayers expected assets acquired during the course of the business to appreciate in value. These assets included the farm, which was purchased for $316,000 in 1991 and which had an appraised value of $409,000 seven years later, and some of the horses, which had increased in value some 18 percent from their purchase price. The fourth factor favored the taxpayers.

5) In evaluating the taxpayers' past success in other businesses, the court weighed the objective facts regarding net losses in a dog-breeding business and antiques store, with the taxpayers' statements that they were "entrepreneurial" and that they closed the other businesses because they were not profitable. The court found other reasons for closing the businesses and said that the mixed results of the taxpayers' other business ventures did not indicate a profit motive. The fifth factor favored the IRS.

6) The court compared the losses recorded during 11 consecutive non-profitable years ($542,751) with the income reported during the same period ($56,010). The court was not persuaded by the taxpayers' explanations for the losses that included a depressed market for Paso Fino horses, the loss of some horses to medical problems, and reliance on a questionable expert. The sixth factor favored the IRS.

7) The taxpayers claimed that they were focusing on producing a national champion Paso Fino, which might have a value of $250,000 or more, and that their 11 consecutive losing years reflect that intent. The court explained that such a belief could indicate a profit motive, but determined that under the facts of the case, such a belief on the part of the taxpayers was too speculative. The court noted that during the years in question the taxpayers did not have breeding stock of sufficient quality to produce a national champion and that they never had shown any of their horses at national shows. The court also noted that the taxpayers' advertising was directed at a local rather than national market. The seventh factor favored the IRS.

8) By using the losses from their Paso Fino operation to reduce their non-farm income, the taxpayers lowered their taxable income by approximately $60,000 a year during the period at issue. The IRS argued that the tax savings, plus the recreational value of the activity, showed a lack of profit motive; the taxpayers countered with the argument that the level of money spent, in comparison to their overall income,

was more than anyone would spend on a hobby. The court found merit in both arguments. The eighth factor favored neither the taxpayers nor the IRS.

9) The IRS argued that the taxpayers loved their horses — which they did not deny — and that they chose Paso Finos because they provided a social outlet for the taxpayers. The IRS also argued that the taxpayers chose Paso Finos, in part, because the husband could ride them despite his bad back and pointed to the taxpayers' e-mail address (Pasolove) as proof of their emotional involvement in the activity. The court apparently agreed, stating that the taxpayers' attachment to their animals "may explain why [the taxpayers] devoted so little effort to culling their herd, improving the quality of their horses, and reducing their operating expenses prior to 1994." The ninth factor favored the IRS.

With six of the nine relevant factors favoring the IRS, two favoring the taxpayers, and one favoring neither, the Tax court ruled against the taxpayers, holding that their Paso Fino operation was not engaged in for profit. The court said that despite some conflicting evidence, their overall conclusion was that the taxpayers "enjoyed breeding and showing their horses and, therefore, were willing to sustain continuing losses, despite the improbability of profit."

This example, like the first, is instructive. Here the taxpayers had no business plan, either before they started buying Paso Finos or after their farm was in operation. They relied on their own limited expertise or occasionally relied on a questionable expert for assistance. They kept records, but did not utilize those records in a way that could have helped them increase the profitability of their operation. They did not sell any horses for several years, then sold only to cull their herd.

It is tempting to see the second example as proof that the IRS will recognize enjoying your horse activity and running it as a business as mutually exclusive, but that is not the case. The Tax Court was careful to explain that deriving personal pleasure from an activity is only one of nine relevant factors and does not preclude a profit motive. It is clear, though, that IRS recognition of a profit motive depends on having all your ducks in a row with a sound and flexible business plan, either personal or outside expertise, comprehensive record-keeping procedures, expert assistance in the business aspects of the operation, and an ongoing (and demonstrable) commitment to turning a profit.

Appearances do matter. If your horse activity looks like a business to an outsider, it is more likely to be treated like one if there is a tax audit.

ACTIVE OR PASSIVE LOSS?

Even if your horse business is conducted with the requisite profit motive, your ability to deduct losses from the operation against other income may be limited if you do not "materially participate" in the activity. If there is no active participation in a business by a taxpayer, losses from the business can be deducted only against income from other "passive" activities and not against salary income, interest income, or income from an activity in which the taxpayer does have active participation.

Such so-called "passive losses" may be carried forward to be used against passive income in subsequent years, and a taxpayer can deduct passive losses in full in the year in which the passive activity is sold or otherwise disposed of.

This provision of the tax code clearly presents potential problems for some horse owners. If you are a limited partner in a partnership that races or shows horses, for example, the IRS will consider your partnership interest to be passive. The same is true for any other business activity in which the taxpayer does not materially participate.

The tax code defines material participation in an activity as involvement by a taxpayer that is "regular, continuous, and substantial." If you spend at least 500 hours on your business during a tax year, you will meet the IRS test for active participation. If you spend less than 100 hours on the business during a year, your participation will not satisfy the IRS threshold.

If you spend more than 100 hours on your business in a year but less than 500 hours, you still may satisfy the IRS test depending on the facts and circumstances of your specific business. You should keep a detailed log of the time you spend on your business. Less than two hours per week will satisfy the 100-hour threshold, and 10 hours per week will meet the 500-hour presumption of material participation. You also should consult an attorney or accountant for advice about what specific activities satisfy the material participation test.

SALES AND USE TAXES

Sales taxes and use taxes are different incarnations of the same creature — a tax paid by the purchaser of specified property or services. The difference between the two depends on the locations of the buyer and seller. If you purchase property from a seller who is doing business in your state, you will be required to pay a percentage of the retail price to the seller, who acts as a tax collector for the state. This is a sales tax and the concept should be familiar unless you happen to live in one of the states with no sales tax.

If, on the other hand, you purchase property from a seller in another state, you may be required to pay a use tax based on a percentage of the retail price. This is a less-familiar concept, one that can result in an unpleasant surprise if you purchase a horse in another state and bring it back to your own state. Without proper planning, you may wind up facing a hefty use-tax liability.

Sales and use taxes are strictly matters of state law, and you should consult with a qualified attorney or tax professional in your jurisdiction for comprehensive planning advice. In general, though, between 15 and 20 states either have no sales/use taxes or make all sales of horses exempt.

Other states, like Kentucky, exempt from taxes the sale or use of some horses. In Kentucky, sales of horses (or interests or shares in horses) used exclusively for breeding are exempt from sales or use taxes. Other states with similar provisions for breeding stock include Arkansas, Colorado, Florida, Georgia, Hawaii, Idaho, Illinois, Kansas, Louisiana, Maryland, Missouri, New Jersey, New Mexico, New York, North Carolina, Utah, Wisconsin, and West Virginia.

Kentucky law also exempts from sales or use taxes stallion services and horses under two years of age at the time of sale. The latter exemption is available when the sale is made to a nonresident of Kentucky and the horse is transported out-of-state immediately after the sale or immediately after training within Kentucky, so long as the horse's post-sale stay in the state is temporary and for training purposes only. A stable owner from New York, for example, does not pay Kentucky sales tax on a yearling purchased at Keeneland provided that the yearling is either shipped immediately out of Kentucky or is shipped out of state following a temporary training period.

Creative tax planning generally is associated with efforts to reduce federal income-tax liability, but state sales- and use-tax statutes also can be a fertile ground for legitimate tax avoidance. For example, Kentucky, California, and some other states that generally impose a use tax (equal to the state sales tax) on horses purchased elsewhere, then brought to the state, make exceptions in certain circumstances.

A horse purchased outside Kentucky then brought into the state within 90 days of the sale generally will be considered as purchased for use within the state and a six-percent use tax will be imposed. Use tax generally would not be imposed on the same horse if it was imported into Kentucky more than 90 days after the purchase, however. Advance planning can save money, and, as always, you should consult an attorney or tax professional in your state for specific advice.

You also should be aware of the risks that go hand in hand

with innovative tax strategies. From 1982 through early 1985, for example, Calumet Farm in Kentucky sold numerous "lifetime breeding rights" in the prominent Thoroughbred stallion Alydar. The breeding rights gave the purchaser a right to breed one mare a year to Alydar plus a second mare in each alternate year throughout the stallion's life. The breeding rights were not shares in Alydar, however, because they specifically did not convey any interest in the horse. The plan, in theory at least, allowed Calumet to exploit the popularity of Alydar without losing ownership interest.

Calumet interpreted sale of these breeding rights as exempt from Kentucky sales tax. Characterizing the breeding rights as almost identical to a share in Alydar, Calumet reasoned that the sales fell under the state sales-tax exemption for sales of "horses, or interests or shares in horses." The state Revenue Cabinet, and eventually the Kentucky Court of Appeals, disagreed. The court upheld the Revenue Cabinet's imposition of a deficiency assessment because purchase of a breeding right was found to be nothing more than payment of a very expensive stud fee, a transaction to which state sales tax specifically applied.

A close reading of your state statutes also may be necessary to learn if your purchases of feed, hay, and farm equipment are subject to state sales and use taxes. In Kentucky, for example, feed for livestock and farm machinery used exclusively in the production of livestock are exempt from the state's six-percent sales tax.

If you think this is a clear-cut benefit for horse owners, however, think again. Kentucky law limits the statutory definition of "livestock" to animals produced for food, and one Kentucky court noted, "Happily, the legendary esteem in which Kentuckians have always held horseflesh has never extended to the dinner table." Feed for cattle is exempt from the sales tax; feed for horses is not, at least in Kentucky where horses, by statutory definition, are not "livestock."

Although sales and use taxes might seem insignificant, at

least when compared with income taxes, you should not ignore the possibilities these taxes offer for tax planning and possible savings.

TWO-FOUR-SIX-EIGHT: HOW DO WE DEPRECIATE?

The Tax Code allows taxpayers operating a business to deduct from gross income "all the ordinary and necessary expenses paid or incurred during the taxable year." Deductible business expenses for a horse business can include wages paid to your employees, the cost of feed and hay, utility bills, veterinary bills, fuel and upkeep expenses for farm vehicles, some transportation costs, interest on business-related indebtedness, and property taxes.

Most big-ticket items such as farm buildings, farm machinery, vehicles, and horses are not considered expenses however, but investments of capital. You still get credit for the purchase price of these things, but the tax treatment is somewhat different. Rather than taking an immediate deduction for the entire cost of the property, you must apportion a certain amount of the price to each year of the item's expected useful life. The process is called depreciation.

The useful life of depreciable farm property varies. Racehorses more than two years old and breeding stock or other horses more than 12 years of age are depreciated over a three-year period; all other horses are depreciated over a seven-year period. Most farm vehicles are depreciated over a five-year period; most farm equipment is depreciated over seven years; and non-residential agricultural buildings are depreciated over 10 or 20 years depending on the type and use of the structure.

The two most common ways to compute depreciation are the simpler "straight-line method" and the "declining balance method," which is used more often because it allocates a higher percentage of the cost to the early years of the property's useful life. The former provides for a depreciation allowance in equal amounts during the property's useful life;

the latter provides for accelerated depreciation during the first years after depreciable property is placed in service.

Consider a $20,000 light-duty farm truck placed into service on January 1, 1995, and depreciated over a five-year period. Using straight-line depreciation, the taxpayer deducts one-fifth of the total cost ($4,000, or 20 percent) each year for five years. Using a declining balance method, on the other hand, the straight-line rate (20 percent) is multiplied by 150 percent (for horses and most other depreciable farm property), and the resulting depreciation rate (30 percent) is applied each year to the unrecovered balance to determine the depreciation allowance for that year. The depreciation allowance will be greater than $4,000 (the straight-line allowance) for the first two years, but less thereafter.

Taxpayers also have the option of writing off, or "expensing," the entire purchase price of horses and other equipment during the first tax year, up to a maximum of $20,000. (This maximum will increase to $24,000 in 2001 and to $25,000 in 2003.) There are some restrictions depending on the amount of depreciable property acquired during the year.

CAPITAL GAINS

You also may be entitled to special tax treatment if you purchase a horse, hold it for a specified period of time, and then sell the animal for a profit. If the horse qualifies, any profits from the sale are taxed at a rate lower than the taxpayer's regular tax rate. If your regular federal tax rate is 15 percent, the capital gains tax rate will be 10 percent. If you are in any other higher federal tax bracket, the capital gains tax rate will be 20 percent.

To qualify, the horse must be held by the taxpayer for 24 months if held for breeding or sporting purposes (including racing and showing). Also, the taxpayer must not keep the horse for the primary purpose of selling the animal to clients. If you lose money on the sale of property that qualifies for capital gains treatment, the loss can offset other long-term capital gains, and if there is a net long-term capital loss, up to $3,000 can be deducted against ordinary income.

If all this is thoroughly confusing and you have neither the time nor the interest to pore through the Tax Code, you should understand why professional tax assistance is vital to the continued success of your horse business.

CHAPTER 6

Winning the Insurance Game

Buying insurance is a lot like placing a bet at the race-track, since both activities involve you making predictions, then backing up those predictions with your money. The fundamental difference is that when you purchase an insurance policy, you are making a bet that you hope to lose.

At the track, the anticipated event is your horse crossing the finish line ahead of the field, and when that happens, you are a winner. If the game is insurance, on the other hand, the anticipated event can be nearly anything — at least anything that has a bad result. A lightning strike that destroys a barn, an accident that seriously injures a boarder, a potential breeding stallion that turns out to be infertile, the unexpected death of a valuable horse are the betting slips of the insurance game. You "win" when nothing bad happens and you don't collect. Peace of mind is the payoff.

Horseplayers are eternal optimists, always looking ahead for the next big winner. Similar optimism for someone in the horse business, at least to the extent that it makes you think nothing bad will happen, can be costly. Stay in the horse business long enough and you, one of your employees or boarders, or a horse in your care will have an accident. Although good management practices can tilt the scales somewhat in your favor, for nearly everyone the ultimate question is not whether an accident will happen but when it will happen. Insurance does not replace good management, but a well-thought-out insurance plan can protect you when, despite your best efforts, something goes wrong.

If there is a trick to winning the insurance game, it is being aware of your insurance needs and buying enough insurance — but no more — than is required to protect your interests. Under-insuring or having no insurance at all will not protect you in the event of a

> ## AT A GLANCE
>
> • A care, custody, or control policy generally protects owners of boarding farms against liability.
>
> • Separate coverage may be required for owners of a commercial riding stable.
>
> • Most liability laws impose a notice requirement on the farm or stable owner.
>
> • Mortality insurance is the most common form of equine insurance.

catastrophe; over-insuring, on the other hand, is a waste of money. A good insurance agent can tailor a plan to your specific circumstances and can be a valuable ally both before and after you submit a claim.

You should choose an insurance agent with the same care you would use in picking any other professional. Personal references may be the best indicator, and if you have friends in the horse business, find out who handles their insurance. Ask questions: Was the agent helpful and knowledgeable, both about insurance matters in general and about the horse business in particular? Were claims handled promptly and fairly? Did they feel that they got value for their insurance dollars?

AN INSURANCE PRIMER — LIABILITY

Most of us are familiar with basic automobile and homeowners insurance, and it is tempting to assume that the standard homeowners policy you probably already have will adequately protect a modest horse business as well. You make this assumption at your own peril.

Homeowners policies generally do not cover liability resulting from business activities, and your insurance carrier almost certainly will adopt a very broad interpretation of "business" when asked to pay a claim relating to your horse operation. It also is possible that your general farm owners policy may include livestock generally, but may specifically exclude horses. A reputable insurance agent should be able to review your current insurance coverage and recommend additional policies to fill in any gaps.

Your agent also may recommend an "umbrella" policy, so named because it covers a host of potential — but typically less likely — sources of liability that may not be addressed and named specifically in your general liability policy. Usually purchased as a supplement to a standard farm owners policy, an umbrella policy provides coverage above and beyond the general policy and usually can be purchased with relatively little additional expense.

Even if your general farm owners policy does cover business activities and does not exclude horses from its coverage, most such insurance policies specifically exclude coverage for horses, equipment, and other property not owned by the insured (you) but that are in your care. In other words, if you are conducting a boarding business or any other type of operation in which you assume the responsibility for a horse belonging to someone else, you should discuss with your agent "care, custody, or control" coverage.

A care, custody, or control policy generally protects a farm owner who boards horses against liability arising from an injury to, or the death of, a horse quartered at the farm. Typical policies also cover the legal expenses incurred as a result of the farm owner's defense of a lawsuit brought as a result of a boarded horse's injury or death. Considering the litigious nature of our society and the often astronomical legal fees that can result from even the successful defense of a lawsuit, such protection should be considered a necessity for any farm owner who accepts responsibility for horses owned by others.

Care, custody, or control coverage also imposes, either directly or implicitly, a duty on the owner of a boarding farm to employ a standard of care at least as good as the standard employed at similar boarding farms. There is no hard and fast definition of an adequate standard of care, and acceptable management practices may vary from state to state. The standard of care on a Thoroughbred boarding farm in Central Kentucky, for example, might be excessive when compared with a Midwestern boarding stable for pleasure horses.

A generally acceptable standard of care likely will include some level of round-the-clock security and supervision of the horses; safely constructed and adequately maintained barns, run-in sheds, fences, and other structures; and provisions for adequate food, water, and veterinary care. An additional consideration is whether the farm owner transports boarded horses, a common scenario at farms that board broodmares that must be shipped to other farms for breeding, or show horses that must be vanned to competitions. If you fail to provide the understood and agreed-upon standard of care either at the farm or in transit, your insurance carrier may refuse to pay in the event of a mishap.

Separate coverage may be required for the owners or operators of a commercial riding stable. A commercial stable policy can be written to cover liability arising during the operation of a business that provides riding lessons or riding clinics, private lessons, or that conducts horse shows on the premises. Such policies typically protect a stable owner who is found to be legally liable for either bodily injury or property damage resulting from the stable operation.

It is important to discuss your insurance needs fully with your agent before an accident happens. Most insurance applications are quite detailed, but if the agent does not know the specific nature of your equine business at the start, you may wind up with unnecessary coverage for activities that do not apply to your business. Even worse, the coverage you get may not be comprehensive enough.

If you tell your agent that you board horses for others, for example, he or she logically might recommend a care, custody, or control policy. But if you neglect to mention that you also give riding lessons to some of the people who board horses at your farm and the agent doesn't ask, you might leave the office without separate stable owner's coverage. This won't be a problem until one of your lesson horses stumbles and tosses his rider, breaking the student's arm, and you find out that you aren't covered for such injuries. You have a right to rely on your insurance agent, but you also should become familiar with your policies to verify that the coverage you get is the coverage you want and need.

Some owners of boarding farms or riding stables attempt to insulate themselves from liability and save money at the same time by foregoing adequate insurance coverage and relying instead on written waivers of liability from their clients. A liability waiver protects the farm or stable owner, at least in theory, by requiring the client to state in writing that he or she both understands the risks inherent in the activity and accepts them.

In practice, however, the effectiveness of a liability waiver depends on several factors. The language used can determine whether the waiver will be enforceable as a defense to a lawsuit, and it is a safer practice to have an attorney experienced in equine matters draft the document rather than use a fill-in-the-blanks form from a book or magazine. Such generic contracts can be useful starting points, but a one-size-fits-all contract almost certainly does not match exactly your particular circumstances.

The laws of your particular state also may affect the enforceability of the waiver, and it is important to keep in mind that a farm or stable owner generally cannot use a contract to eliminate liability for his or her own negligence or for that of the employees. This is an important consideration since many liability insurance policies can be written to cover all but intentional or malicious acts.

Most states also have in effect statutes that limit the liability of a farm owner or equine activity sponsor, and you should become familiar with the laws in your particular state. A lawyer, who already should be a part of your management team, can help here, too. These liability laws generally recognize that horse-related activities have a certain amount of built-in risk, and they restrict the right of a person to sue a farm or stable owner for injuries suffered as a result of participation in the activity.

Most liability laws impose a notice requirement on the farm or stable owner. In Kentucky, for example, a farm or stable owner must post a conspicuous notice warning clients and others that there are inherent risks associated with equine activities and that anyone taking part in the activity assumes the risk. Without the notice, which also must be included in written contracts and liability waivers, a farm owner or activity sponsor does not gain the benefit of the law.

You should include properly drafted liability waivers in your contracts, and you should understand and follow the requirements of your state equine liability laws. Neither, however, should be relied upon as a substitute for adequate liability insurance. Instead, waivers and state liability laws should be seen as the front-line defenses against a finding of liability, with your insurance coverage serving as the ultimate protection for your business.

AN INSURANCE PRIMER — MORTALITY

Unlike liability insurance, the purpose of which is to protect you against liability for bodily injury to others or for the loss of their animals or property, equine mortality insurance provides a mechanism to recoup at least some of an owner's investments of time and money when a horse dies. The most common form of equine insurance, mortality insurance can be purchased as either "full mortality" or "limited mortality." The former, which covers death of a horse either directly or indirectly from accident, illness, or disease, is the more comprehensive and, thus, the more expensive. The latter provides coverage for a limited range of situations and consequently is much less expensive.

A peculiarity of most equine mortality policies, one that has led to numerous misunderstandings, bad feelings, and a substantial amount of litigation, involves the determination of the insured animal's value at death. Most equine insurance underwriters initially insure a horse for a value determined by the owner, with the insurance premiums set accordingly — the higher the stated value, the higher the premium. Most mortality policies only require that the carrier actually pay the fair market value of the horse when it dies, however.

Problems arise because the value of a horse can change dramatically and quickly during its life. If the insurance coverage is not changed periodically to reflect fluctuations in the animal's value, an owner who legitimately insured a national champion show horse for $100,000 at the height of the gelding's success and paid premiums on that basis may receive substantially less than the anticipated $100,000 when the horse dies several years into his retirement. Understandably, and probably unnecessarily, the owner will feel cheated.

The logic of the practice is inescapable, at least from the insurance company's point of view — a retired gelding with no breeding or resale value is worth substantially less than a successful show horse, regardless of the premiums paid. The practice of limiting recovery to fair market value also discourages unscrupulous owners from over-insuring a horse then killing the animal to collect the insurance, schemes that have made national headlines in recent years.

Again, it is important for you to maintain a continuing dialogue with your insurance agent, both to determine the type and amount of coverage you need initially and to evaluate whether your insurance needs have changed. Assume for a moment that you have insured your show horse for

$100,000, with premiums based on that valuation. If you attempt to sell your horse at public auction with a $100,000 reserve (the minimum amount you will take for the animal), and the bidding fails to reach the reserve figure, your insurance carrier probably will take the highest legitimate bid ($60,000, for example) as the animal's current fair market value. If the animal dies the next day, your insurance probably will pay only $60,000, regardless of your higher estimation of value when the insurance was purchased.

The same thing will happen if you enter your insured Thoroughbred in a claiming race, where anyone willing to pay the claiming price set for horses in the race can buy your horse. No matter what you estimated the horse's value to be when you purchased the mortality policy, in the insurance company's eyes the animal's fair market value will be his claiming price in his most recent race. This does not mean, by the way, that you can insure a horse for $10,000, then enter him in a race for $50,000 claimers and collect the higher amount if he dies. All mortality policies set the maximum amount to be paid by the company as the insured value stated in the policy. The company may pay less, but never more, than the agreed-upon insured value of your horse.

Your agent may be able to help you determine the proper value to place on your horse, but you should not rely exclusively on the agent's advice. A potential conflict of interest exists when an insurance agent, whose commission is based on the premiums you pay, is asked to determine the value of the horse to be insured, a figure that will establish the premium amount.

The purchase price at public auction is a good indicator of a horse's fair market value. Establishing a value is more problematic if you purchased the horse privately and even more difficult if the horse is one that you bred and raised yourself. An appraisal by a reputable bloodstock agent, comparison with auction prices for horses with similar bloodlines and performance records, and advice from other breeders may help you strike a balance between having too much and not enough mortality insurance.

A COMMON GROUND

The most heart-wrenching decision that a horse owner must make is whether an animal's condition warrants euthanasia. Although the ultimate choice obviously involves both you and your veterinarian, the insurance carrier also has an interest if there is mortality insurance on your horse, and your mortality policy almost certainly includes a requirement that the carrier be notified immediately if the horse suffers an injury or illness.

A strict reading of the notice provision requires the owner to notify the insurance company of every accident or illness, no matter how minor. You certainly should notify the carrier of a condition so serious that it may necessitate euthanasia, and failure to notify the company of all injuries or illness may give the company grounds to refuse to pay. The purpose of insurance is to eliminate risk; failure to follow a requirement of your mortality policy simply creates an additional risk of loss and is not a sound management practice.

Disputes may develop but, in practice, rarely do in the event of a disagreement between your veterinarian and the veterinarian acting on behalf of the insurer about whether a horse's condition warrants immediate euthanasia or whether time should be allowed for a possible recovery.

To assist veterinarians facing such a situation, the American Association of Equine Practitioners several years ago adopted guidelines and justifications for euthanasia. When deciding whether a horse should be put down, a veterinarian should consider the following:

1. whether the condition is chronic and incurable;

2. whether the horse has a hopeless prognosis for life as a result of the immediate condition;

3. whether the horse is a hazard to himself or to his handlers;

4. whether the horse will require continuous medication to relieve pain for the remainder of his life.

The AAEP also recommends that "justification for euthanasia of a horse for humane reasons should be based on medical and not economic considerations; and, further the same criteria should be applied to all horses regardless of age, sex or potential value."

The AAEP guidelines and justification for euthanasia do not address specific situations. They do make it possible for both your veterinarian and the insurance carrier's veterinarian to evaluate the condition of your horse from the same frame of reference.

AN INSURANCE PRIMER — OTHER OPTIONS

Many other types of insurance are available and should be considered based on your individual circumstances. Various kinds of fertility insurance are available, including coverage for new stallions that pays if a certain proportion of mares bred to the stallion during his first year of stud duty do not get in foal. Mare owners can insure their broodmares against either failing to conceive or losing the foal, coverage that gains importance if the mare is being bred to a stallion on a "no guarantee" basis.

Health insurance that covers veterinary charges for illness or accident, surgical insurance that covers emergency surgery and post-operative care, loss-of-use insurance, and coverage for tack and equipment also are available. Insurance plans are limited only by the imagination of the agent and the budget of the insured.

MAKING SENSE OF THE INDECIPHERABLE

Discovery by archaeologists of the Rosetta stone in 1799, with its parallel inscriptions in Greek, Egyptian, and demotic characters, allowed scientists for the first time to translate ancient Egyptian picture writing. While many insurance policies may seem as incomprehensible as Egyptian hieroglyphics, at least at first glance, you can learn the basics of your coverage with just a little work.

A typical equine mortality policy may contain the following sections:

1. **Definitions**—Basic terms are defined in this section of the policy, including "you" and "your" for the insured and "we," "us," and "our" for the insurance company. Other necessary terms, such as the insurance company's definition of "fair market value," may be found here as well.

2. **Insuring Agreement**—This portion of the policy represents the company's agreement to provide the insurance coverage set out in the policy so long as the insured pays the required premiums and complies with the other terms of the policy. This agreement by the company to provide insurance, if you perform certain obligations, is the heart of the contract and allows for enforcement in court — if you have done everything required in the agreement.

3. **Coverages**—Here can be found the types of situations in which the insurance company will pay. With a full mortality policy, for example, the carrier is insuring the specified horse, or horses, against death that is the direct or indirect result of accident, illness, or disease. For a limited mortality policy, the company insures the specified animal or animals against death resulting from specific stated causes, which may vary from policy to policy. A careful reading of this portion of the policy is necessary to understand what your insurance does and does not cover.

4. **Payment of Loss**—Here the company sets out in detail the method of valuation of the insured animal. If the policy provides "fair market value" coverage, for example, that provision will be stated in this section of the policy. Knowing how the company will determine the value of your animal and, thus, the amount that will be paid if the horse died will help prevent misunderstandings.

5. **Exclusions**—One of the most important parts of the policy, this section explains the situations that specifically

preclude recovery. Typical exclusions include death resulting from intentional or willful acts or omissions by the horse's owner, war, intentional slaughter, some surgical procedures, and administration of drugs under certain circumstances.

6. **Conditions**—This is generally the most lengthy section of the policy, addressing a variety of situations that may affect the coverage. Conditions often include a requirement that you must disclose pre-existing illnesses or injuries suffered by the horse prior to the application for insurance; responsibilities and obligations of the horse owner (including a duty to notify the insurance company in the event of accident or illness); an agreement to submit disputes to arbitration; conditions under which the policy may be canceled by either party; and modifications and extensions of the coverage.

Interpreting an insurance policy can appear daunting, but with a little homework you can understand both the nature and the limits of your coverage.

CHAPTER 7

Alternative Dispute Resolution

"*I'LL SEE YOU IN COURT!*" More and more, these are the parting words in a dispute between friends or business associates. Oftentimes, though, the obvious response to a disagreement — filing a lawsuit — is not the best response. Hiring a lawyer and going to court are stressful, expensive, and time consuming, even if you eventually win the lawsuit, and a growing number of people are seeking an alternative approach to dispute resolution.

The options vary, from binding arbitration to mediation to negotiation, but all types of alternative dispute resolution have in common the goal of a faster, more economical, and less complicated solution to a disagreement. Consider the following:

After a lengthy search for an equitation mount for your daughter, a novice rider, you find what appears to be the ideal horse. Advertised as a proven campaigner on the "A" hunter circuit, the 13-year-old gelding is a "push-button horse" that also is perfectly sound, at least according to his trainer. Your daughter likes the horse, they seem to get along during a brief tryout, and you make the purchase.

A few weeks later, during a training session, the gelding becomes seriously lame. After examining radiographs, your veterinarian diagnoses a chronic ankle problem that in his opinion has been present for several years. Your daughter's medal hopes are dashed and she is devastated, your bank account has taken a major hit, and you are looking for someone to blame. The gelding's former owner does not admit any fault and refuses to take the gelding back.

While it may be tempting to visit your lawyer and sue, there might be a better way to deal with the problem. Rather than go to court, you and the seller can agree to bring in an impartial third party to help resolve

AT A GLANCE

- Arbitration, mediation, and negotiation are forms of alternative dispute resolution.

- The conditions of sale of many public auction companies contain arbitration clauses.

- When choosing a mediator, look for someone with familiarity with the horse business.

the disagreement. If the third party actually makes a decision, usually binding on the parties, the process is called arbitration; if the third party merely attempts to facilitate an agreement between the parties, the process is called mediation. Either way, you and the seller are taking part in a process known as alternative dispute resolution (ADR). While not yet sending the country's lawyers into mass early retirement, ADR quickly is becoming a viable and accepted way to settle disputes outside a courtroom.

The advantages are numerous:

• ADR generally results in a resolution to a dispute much faster than a lawsuit. This can be important when the subject of the dispute, the show horse in the example above, for example, is a living creature with a limited number of productive years. As anyone who has been a party to litigation is aware, the wheels of justice turn slowly (if at all), and it easily can take years for a lawsuit to make its way from service of the initial complaint, to trial, through appeal, to a final decision.

ADR proceedings also can be more convenient than court proceedings. Because the parties and the arbitrator or mediator can schedule their own conferences without reference to a judge's nearly always crowded docket, the parties' schedules generally can be accommodated.

• ADR is cheaper than a lawsuit, at least in theory. Because attorneys often are not involved and because there generally is not extensive discovery or testimony by expensive experts, arbitration or mediation is expected to cost less than traditional judicial avenues. There are fees associated with ADR, however, and anticipated savings sometimes do not materialize.

• There is more privacy for the parties. First, ADR generally provides for limited discovery. After a lawsuit is filed, the parties have the right to discovery, the process by which each party can obtain information on a wide range of topics from the opposing party. Discovery, which can include written questions from one party to another, depositions, and medical examinations, is expensive and time consuming, and in many instances the process can be extremely intrusive. ADR thus may be attractive to a person who does not want details of his or her business or personal life revealed to others.

Second, with few exceptions, court records and documents generated during the course of a lawsuit — including the trial proceedings themselves — are open and available to the public. The owner of a breeding stallion, for example, might prefer to keep a dispute about the fertility of the horse out of the public eye as much as possible. Unlike the trappings of a lawsuit, ADR negotiations are private.

• With ADR, the parties frequently can have their dispute addressed by someone with expertise in the field. One of the often-cited virtues of the American jury system is trial by a jury of one's peers, which means a decision by a representative cross section of your community. It does not mean a jury composed of other horse people, and your jury may or may not understand the issues at the heart of the dispute. A jury trial might become problematic when the issue is interpretation of a complex stallion syndicate agreement, for example, and the jury has no specialized knowledge of the horse business. A bench trial, in which there is no jury and the judge makes the final decision, may be no better, depending on the individual judge's expertise.

ADR, on the other hand, offers at least a good chance that the decision maker (in the case of arbitration) or the facilitator (in the case of mediation) will understand the issues. Good examples are the compulsory arbitration clauses found in the conditions of sale of many public auction companies. At Keeneland in Lexington, Kentucky, for example, a buyer and seller in dispute about a horse's wind (air capacity) are required to submit the question to a panel of three veterinarians. Unlike the parties in the example at the beginning of this chapter that could agree to seek a non-judicial solution to their disagreement as an alternative to a lawsuit, the buyer and seller of the horse with a supposed wind problem have no choice. Going to court is not an option for them.

The process works like this: If the buyer discovers a potential problem with a horse's wind within a set period of time after the hammer falls (which typically is quite short), the buyer notifies the sales company. The company provides to the parties a list of five veterinarians, with the buyer and seller each given an opportunity to strike one of the names off the list. The remaining three veterinarians examine the horse and make a determination about the alleged problem. The decision by the panel of veterinarians is binding. This is an example of compulsory arbitration, in which both the buyer and seller are obligated to resolve any disputes by non-judicial means.

Despite the obvious advantages, ADR is not the best solution for all disputes, nor is it always the best choice for the parties. Although an abbreviated discovery process generally is seen as an advantage offered by ADR, there could be times when extensive discovery might be necessary for a full and fair resolution of the dispute. A dispute arising from the alleged negligent handling of a boarder's horse, for example, may depend on information that shows a pattern of similar conduct on the part of the farm's owners or employees. In-depth discovery probably cannot be accomplished outside a lawsuit.

There also are two sides to the somewhat more relaxed nature of ADR negotiations. Although the formality and red tape of a court proceeding can be intimidating and at times appear to bring the process to a grinding halt, the procedural safeguards of a courtroom protect the rights of the parties. They should not be dispensed with lightly.

Finally, depending on the nature of the dispute and whether the parties decide to involve lawyers and experts, the savings in money and time expected with ADR may not materialize.

Although ADR generally is regarded as a quicker, cheaper, and more convenient way to settle disputes than going to court, the best course of action is to avoid controversy in the first place.

ADR 101

Alternative dispute resolution is a comprehensive term that encompasses all non-judicial ways to resolve a dispute. The most common forms of ADR are arbitration, mediation, and negotiation.

Arbitration involves the submission of a dispute to a neutral third party, the arbitrator (or, in some cases, a panel of arbitrators). After giving both parties the opportunity to present their respective cases, the arbitrator makes a decision that generally will be binding. Arbitration can be "voluntary," in which case the parties agree to the process and also generally have a hand in the selection of the arbitrator, or "compulsory," in which a resistant party is forced to participate either by law or contract.

Compulsory arbitration traditionally has been associated

with state laws that require arbitration of labor disputes that involve public employees. To avoid a crippling strike, for example, municipal transit workers and their union may be required by law to submit wage disputes to arbitration, with both the union and the city bound by the arbitrator's decision.

Consent to submit a dispute to binding arbitration also can be written into a contract. Such an arbitration clause can have broad, inclusive language that covers many — or all — of the disputes arising from the contract, or the clause can be narrowly drafted to address only one or two specific issues. Because an arbitration clause amounts to an enforceable promise by the parties to submit disputes to ADR rather than go to court, and because courts generally will enforce such clauses, it is important that you read and understand all the terms of a contract before you sign.

If you do not understand everything written in a contract, don't sign it until you do. Needless to say, never sign a contract with blanks that the other party promises "will be filled in later." Finally, if you ignore our advice and sign a contract without reading it, your failure to do so will not be a defense in a legal action. Courts generally — and logically — presume that anyone who signed a contract did so only after reading it first, and you may be bound by an arbitration clause you did not realize existed.

This may sound far-fetched, but you already may have been exposed to and bound by a binding arbitration clause if you bought a horse at public auction. Nearly every auction has published conditions of sale that the seller and buyer agree to, either explicitly or by virtue of their participation in the sale. Many of these Conditions of Sale include one or more arbitration clauses that come into play in the event of a dispute over an animal's condition.

Following an arbitration award, the prevailing party can go to court to enforce the decision in the same manner in which a jury verdict is enforced.

A more common type of ADR is mediation, in which an impartial third party helps the parties reach a mutually acceptable solution to a dispute. Unlike an arbitrator, a mediator does not render a binding decision and the result of a mediation session generally cannot be enforced in court by either party. Among the principal types of organized alternative dispute resolution, non-binding mediation is the preferred choice.

In a 1999 survey conducted by *The National Law Journal* and the American Arbitration Association, mediation was favored over arbitration by a large majority of attorneys who said they used mediation for the resulting savings in time and money. Another less-obvious benefit from mediation cited by a number of the attorneys surveyed who favored that avenue of dispute resolution is the increased chance of maintaining a working relationship between the parties in dispute. Lawsuits tend to bring out the worst in everyone involved and the resulting animosity sometimes can be avoided, or at least minimized, by using ADR.

Many cities have mediation services that for a fee help parties in dispute work things out on their own. The success of mediation primarily depends on the willingness of the parties to make good faith efforts to resolve the dispute, a process that often starts when the parties must reach agreement about selecting the mediator.

When considering a mediator, you should evaluate both his or her general qualifications and training, plus the mediator's familiarity with the horse business. Even a skilled mediator will have difficulty helping parties resolve a breeding contract dispute, for example, if he does not understand the usage in the horse business of terms such as "live foal" and "no guarantee."

A third kind of ADR is direct negotiation between the parties involved in the dispute. Negotiation is the usual first attempt to reach a solution to a disagreement, and it is the last opportunity for the parties to reach a resolution without involving someone else, either a lawyer or a third-party arbitrator or mediator.

CHAPTER 8

Resources

Having gotten this far, you should be familiar with the idea that the success of your horse business will be greatly enhanced if you have a team of experts on your side. Collectively, these professionals can be your most valuable resource. Not that you cannot succeed strictly on your own; you can, but why insist on reinventing the wheel at every turn. Instead, learn to rely on professionals whose expertise can help you reach your goals.

One of the most important ongoing relationships you have is with your veterinarian, who can treat sudden illness and injury and, just as important, also help you practice preventive medicine. The same can be said for a good farrier.

Less obvious, but in some circumstances just as important, are an attorney and accountant, preferably with expertise in the horse business. If you are fortunate, you live in an area with a horse population large enough to support veterinarians, attorneys, and accountants with specialized equine practices. More likely, though, you do not, and you will have to locate general practitioners willing to learn about horses in general and your business in particular. Wherever you live, advice from others in the horse business generally will be your best guide to finding competent professionals.

Local colleges and universities also can be an important

source of information and referrals. Every state has a land-grant university with a web of state and county extension specialists whose job it is to gather and disseminate information on a wide variety of topics. A veterinary school also can be a valuable resource if you and your local veterinarian are faced with diagnosing and treating a complicated condition. Keep in mind, though, that no one can diagnose your horse's illness over the telephone, and you should not ask anyone to do so.

> ## AT A GLANCE
>
> • Advice from other horse owners is usually your best guide to finding competent professionals.
>
> • General and breed-specific organizations can be good sources of information.
>
> • The Internet can provide valuable information on the horse business, but it should not replace your local professionals.

Your banker can be an important resource when you need a loan to establish or expand your horse business and also to help you set up a line of credit. Horse businesses, even the profitable ones, generally do not have a steady cash flow and a line of credit can help you weather the inevitable periods when the money coming in does not equal the money that must be paid out.

You should explore sources of general business information, such as the Service Corps of Retired Executives (SCORE) and the Small Business Administration. Although you probably will not be able to get specialized help from groups like these, there are basic business principles that are applicable to all businesses.

General and breed-specific organizations also can be valuable sources of information. The American Horse Council is a national organization based in Washington, D.C,. that serves primarily as a national lobbying group that represents everyone in the horse business. The AHC also publishes a comprehensive tax guide for horse businesses, and membership includes periodical tax and general information newsletters. The AHC can be contacted at 1700 K Street NW, Suite 300,

Washington, DC 20006, by e-mail at ahc@horsecouncil.org or on the Internet at http://www.horsecouncil.org.

Many states also have their own horse councils that represent the interests of horse enthusiasts in the state legislature and also offer educational opportunities. If your state has a horse council, support its efforts. The American Horse Council can help with contact information for your state. Also investigate breed organizations and local riding clubs. Many offer speakers and educational seminars that can be useful, even if you don't raise Quarter Horses or ride dressage. The IRS expects you to conduct your horse activity in a businesslike manner, and one way to do that is to take every available opportunity to increase your knowledge.

For many, the most easily accessible source of information about horses — and just about anything else — is the Internet. Start your search engine, type in a few pertinent terms, and within seconds you have at your fingertips the varied opinions of individuals and organizations all around the world. Almost instantaneous information on nearly any subject is a benefit of the Internet, but also its biggest weakness. Anyone can say just about anything on the Internet, with no outside agency checking facts or making certain that a product can do what the manufacturer says it can.

Not everyone espousing a theory on the Internet is a crackpot or a quack, but some are, and it can be difficult to tell the difference. You can pick up valuable information about veterinary medicine on the Internet, for example, but you have no way of knowing whether the treatment is likely to help — or harm — your horse. Just as your local extension specialist or a faculty member at a veterinary school cannot diagnose your horse's condition over the telephone, you cannot expect a reliable diagnosis on the Internet from someone who doesn't know your horse or your particular situation.

It is tempting to second-guess your veterinarian, farrier, attorney, or your accountant, especially when something goes wrong, and the Internet gives you almost countless ways to do that. You should recognize that there is no substitute for personal attention from a professional. The Internet can provide valuable information you can discuss with your team of experts, but you should resist the temptation to be a Monday morning quarterback by seeking a second (or third, or fourth) Internet opinion from someone who never has examined your horse or seen your business.

Books and magazines are valuable sources of information, far too numerous to list here. Like the Internet, however, you should take what you read with a large grain of salt. No book, this one included, can provide information specific to your particular situation, and no book or magazine article is intended to replace a relationship with a professional familiar with your unique situation. Books, magazines, and the Internet are starting points for discussion with your own veterinarian, farrier, or attorney, but they cannot, and should not, replace your local professionals.

OWNERSHIP OPTIONS AT A GLANCE

Form of ownership	Taxed at entity level?	Participate in management?	No. of owners	Personal Liability?	Duration?	Available in all 50 states?
Sole proprietorship	No	Yes	1	Yes	Life	Yes
C corporation	Yes	Yes	No limit	No	Indefinite	Yes
S corporation	No	Yes	≤ 35	Limited	Indefinite	Yes
General Partnership	No, but does file tax return	Yes	No limit	Yes	Indefinite[1]	Yes
Limited Partnership	No, but does file tax return	Only General Partners Participate	≥1 general partner, no limit on # of limited partners	General partners—Yes Limited partners—No	Indefinite[1]	Yes
Limited Liability Company	No, but does file tax return	Yes	No limit	N/A	Indefinite	No
Limited Liability Partnership	No, but does file tax return	Yes	≥1 general partner, no limit on # of limited partners	for own actions only	Indefinite[1]	No

1 Partnership agreement will specify conditions that will cause partnership to terminate.

Accrual method of accounting — A method of accounting in which income is reported when it is earned, even if the money is received at a later date, and in which expenses are reported when they are incurred, even if they are not actually paid until later. Businesses that sell equipment or supplies are required to use the accrual method.

Active loss — Losses recorded by an activity in which a taxpayer actively participates. (See passive loss.)

Age Discrimination in Employment Act — Federal legislation that makes it illegal to discriminate against a person on the basis of age.

Alternative dispute resolution (ADR) — A collective term for various non-judicial ways to settle disputes. These include arbitration (in which a dispute is submitted to an impartial third party, whose decision is binding on the parties), mediation (in which an impartial third party helps resolve the disputes, but whose decision is not binding), and direct negotiation (in which the two parties in dispute try and resolve disagreements between themselves).

Americans with Disabilities Act — Federal legislation that makes it illegal to discriminate against an individual on the basis of disability.

Attractive nuisance — Attractive nuisance is a legal concept addressing a person who maintains or creates some condition on his or her property that would be both attractive and dangerous to children. Under such a situation, the property owner has a duty to take reasonable precautions to prevent harm to children who might be attracted to the dangerous condition. Horses in a pasture may or may not be considered an attractive nuisance, depending on your state laws.

Agister's lien — An agister is a person who boards horses or other livestock for a fee. An agister's lien is the right a farm owner has to retain and sell an animal to recover a board bill following a default by the animal's owner. Requirements for, and the rights arising from, an agister's lien vary from state to state.

Attorney-in-fact — An attorney-in-fact is a person who has legal permission to act for another.

Bailee — A bailee is the person to whom personal property is delivered under a contract of bailment. In other words, when you board your horse at another person's farm, the farm owner is the bailee.

Bailment— A temporary delivery of goods or personal property, such as a horse, from one person to another. In a boarding situation, the owner of the horse is the bailor; the owner of the boarding farm is the bailee. The bailee generally is responsible for exercising reasonable care in boarding the animal.

Bailor— A bailor is the party who delivers personal property to another under a contract of bailment. In other words, when you board your horse at another person's farm, you are the bailor.

Balance sheet — An accounting tool that summarizes the assets and liabilities of a business or individual.

Bill of sale — A written document outlining the conditions of sale.

Budget — An accounting and planning tool that allows you to make estimates about upcoming income and expenses.

Business expense — Ordinary and necessary expenses incurred as a result of operating a business. For a horse business, such expenses generally include wages paid to employees, the cost of feed and hay, utility bills, veterinary bills, fuel and upkeep for vehicles, some transportation costs, interest on business-related loans, and property taxes.

Capital gain (or loss) — Gains (or losses) resulting from the sale of capital assets, which are property used in a business. If a transaction qualifies, you may be eligible for special tax treatment on the gain (or loss).

Care, custody, and control policy — A type of insurance policy that protects a farm owner who boards horses for others against liability arising from injury to, or the death of, a horse boarded at the farm.

Cash flow projection — An accounting tool used to predict the amount of cash expected or needed at a particular time, based on certain assumptions about your business. A cash flow projection is a useful planning tool.

Cash method of accounting — The simplest and most common accounting system, in which income is reported when the money is received and expenses are reported when they are actually paid. Many businesses can use the cash method if the business does not maintain an inventory.

Choice of law — Contracts generally include a clause stating which state's laws will govern any disputes arising from the contract. A choice of law clause is most important when the parties are from different states or countries.

Commercial stable policy — A type of insurance policy that covers liability arising from the operation of a riding stable where lessons are given or where horse shows are held.

Common law — Rules and principles that arise from general usage over time or from judicial decisions. Common law principles are different from statutory law, which arises from legislative action.

Consideration — Consideration most often arises in the context of a written or oral contract and is the inducement to form the contract. When a contract states that "in consideration of the sum of $ _____, paid by the owner (of the horse) to the operator (of the farm), the operator agrees to board the horse," or something similar, the owner's agreement to pay board and the farm operator's agreement to board the horse are the consideration for the contract. Consideration is a necessary element of a valid and legally binding contract.

Consignment fee — Many sales companies require that the seller pay a fee before a horse is accepted for sale. This is a consignment fee.

Contract — In its simplest form, a contract is an agreement between parties that creates obligations and responsibilities. In actual practice, a contract includes a variety of clauses and information not directly related to the business transaction. The contract terms should be tailored to the facts and circumstances of the individual business transaction.

Corporation — A corporation is a legal entity created under the authority of a state's laws. The corporation is owned by investor shareholders, who put at risk the amount of their investment but who generally are not personally liable for debts incurred by the business. Corporations can be one of two types, "C" and "S" corporations, whose differences include tax treatment by the Internal Revenue Service.

Current assets — Assets of a business or individual that will be received in cash, or converted to cash, within one year.

Current liabilities — Liabilities of a business or individual that are payable within one year.

Depreciation — When the cost of an asset, such as a racehorse or a piece of farm equipment, is spread out over the expected useful life of the asset.

Disclaimer — A statement by a seller attempting to sell a horse without the usual warranties.

Durable power of attorney — A durable power of attorney is identical to a general power of attorney, except that it remains in force after the principal becomes disabled.

Employee handbook — A written manual provided by an employer to an employee setting out the rights and obligations of the parties.

Employment at will — A common employment relationship in which an employee can be fired without cause, provided the firing does not violate a legal prohibition against discrimination.

Employment contract — An agreement, either written or oral, setting out the rights and responsibilities of an employer and employee.

Equal Pay Act — Federal legislation making it illegal for an employer to discriminate based on an employee's gender in the payment of wages for similar jobs.

Equine law — Something of a misnomer, equine law refers to the application of a variety of legal disciplines, including contract law, tax law, liability law, and estate planning, to horse owners and horse businesses.

Exculpatory clause — A portion of a contract that releases one of the parties from liability for his or her wrongful acts. A typical exculpatory clause includes language similar to the following: "The farm owner shall not be liable for any injury or damage to the horse, including but not limited to loss by fire, theft, disease, accident, escape, injury, or death. Enforceability of an exculpatory clause depends on a number of factors, including state equine liability laws.

Express warranty — A positive statement of fact made by a seller to a buyer. Not all statements create a warranty, however; called "puffery," some statements are so outrageous that a buyer cannot reasonably believe them.

Fair market value — The price that a horse or other property would bring in a market of willing buyers and sellers.

Fertility insurance — Insurance coverage for breeding animals. Stallions can be insured against infertility and broodmares can be insured against either failing to conceive or failing to carry a foal to term.

General partnership — An unincorporated business owned by two or more individuals. All general partners share profits, losses, and management responsibilities equally.

Hobby loss — A hobby loss is a loss resulting from an avocation (an activity not undertaken for profit) rather than a business and generally is not deductible.

Hold harmless clause — A portion of a contract whereby one party releases the other party from liability arising from the contractual relationship. A hold harmless clause in a boarding contract will contain language similar to the following: "The owner (of the horse) shall be solely responsible for all acts and behavior of the horse, and hereby agrees to indemnify and hold the farm owner harmless for all damages sustained or suffered by reason of the boarding of the horse and for any claims or injuries arising out of, or related in any way to, the horse."

Honorary trust — A provision of a will may create an honorary trust, which imposes a non-legal obligation on the named trustee. A court can honor an honorary trust if the provision does not violate law or public policy.

Immigration and Naturalization Service — A federal agency that regulates foreign nationals living and working in the United States.

Implied warranty — Promises that come into being without an express statement of fact by the seller. They include warranty of title (by offering a horse for sale, the seller implies that he has the legal right to sell the animal), warranty of merchantability (which applies to sellers who hold themselves out top be an expert and which requires the horse to be generally suitable for the purposes for which it is being sold), and warranty of fitness for a particular purpose (which applies when the seller knows of particular requirements of a buyer, and when the buyer relies on the seller to provide such an animal).

INS Form I-9 — Required verification that an employee can work legally in the United States.

Irrevocable trust — An irrevocable trust is established during the lifetime of the maker of the trust but cannot be altered by the maker. Use of an irrevocable trust may reduce federal estate tax liability.

Joint and Several Liability — A legal concept in which responsibilities and liabilities are shared by two or more persons, both collectively and individually. If two partners are jointly and severally liable for a partnership's debts, for example, and one of the partners does not pay, the other partner can be held responsible for the total debt.

Lease — An agreement under which the owner of property (a horse) grants to another person the right to possess and use the property for a pre-determined period of time in exchange for periodic payments of a specified sum. There is no change of ownership when a horse is leased.

Legal audit — Many attorneys recommend a periodic review of the operation of a farm or business. The purpose is to determine whether contracts are being used, terms need to be revised, proper records are being kept, local equine liability laws are being followed, bookkeeping is adequate, labor laws are being followed, insurance coverage is adequate, and whether to review anything else related to the general legal health of the business. A legal audit is preventive medicine for a business.

Lessee — The party who rents the horse (or other real or personal property) from another person.

Lessor — The owner of the horse (or other property) being leased.

Liability — Liability refers to a person's legal (and sometimes moral or ethical) responsibility for his or her actions. A person who negligently allows another person's property to suffer damage is liable for that damage.

Liability law — State laws that attempt to limit a farm owner's liability for injuries to individuals taking part in farm activities. Nearly all states have such laws, although the requirements for notice vary from state to state.

Liability waiver — A written statement by a person participating in an activity in which the participant acknowledges that the activity has inherent risks and that he or she accepts those risks. A liability waiver, which may or may not be enforceable in your state, helps insulate a farm owner from liability.

Limited liability company — A business entity available in some but not all states that combines aspects of a partnership (pass-through taxation) and a corporation (limited liability).

Limited liability partnership — A relatively new business entity similar to a general partnership, except that the individual partners are not personally liable for the actions of the other partners. This type of ownership is not recognized in all states.

Limited partnership — An unincorporated business owned by two or more individuals, at least one of whom serves as a general partner and at least one of whom serves as a limited partner. The general partner (or partners) operates the business and is liable personally for the debts of the business. The limited partner (or partners) contributes a specific amount of capital to the business, the amount of which establishes the limit of his or her personal liability of business debts. The limited partners do not take an active part in the operation of the business.

Limited power of attorney — A limited power of attorney authorizes one person to act on behalf of another only in certain circumstances, or for a specific period of time.

Living will — A document that allows a person to make advance decisions about health care that will take effect if and when the person becomes incapacitated. A living will also allows a person to designate as his or her health care surrogate another person who will have the authority to make medical decisions for the person making the living will.

Minimum wage — The least amount of money that can be paid legally to a worker.

Mortality insurance — Insurance coverage on the life of an animal. Such coverage can be either "full mortality," which is more expensive and covers death from any cause, or "limited mortality," which covers only death from specified causes.

Occupational Health and Safety Act (OSHA) — Federal legislation designed to protect workers from dangerous jobs and working conditions. Many states also have their own safety and health regulations.

Oral contract — An agreement that has not been reduced to writing. An oral contract can be enforced in court, provided there is proof of both the existence of the contract and its terms.

Partnership — An unincorporated business entity composed of a group of individuals who have joined together to pursue a common business interest.

Passive loss — A passive loss results when an activity in which the taxpayer does not materially participate loses money. The Internal Revenue Service limits the deductibility of passive losses.

Power of attorney — Also called a "general power of attorney," a power of attorney is a legal document that authorizes one person to act on behalf of another. A general power of attorney does not continue in force if the principal becomes disabled. (See durable power of attorney, springing power of attorney, and limited power of attorney.)

Profit and loss statement — An accounting tool that shows the net earnings (gross earnings less expenses) during a specified period of time. Also called a P&L or income statement.

Revocable trust — Also known as a "living trust," a revocable trust takes effect during the lifetime of the maker of the trust but can be modified by the maker during his or her lifetime. It helps delay probate, making it useful for some estate planning purposes, but use of a revocable trust will not reduce federal estate tax liability.

Right of survivorship — Right of survivorship refers to the right of one person to the property of another, upon the latter's death. When a couple holds title to property jointly with right of survivorship, for example, title will pass to the husband upon the wife's death.

Sales tax — A state-imposed tax based on a percentage of the purchase price of items purchased within the taxing state.

Security interest — An interest in personal property, such as a horse, that guarantees payment or performance of an obligation. If the boarding farm has obtained a security interest in a horse being boarded at the facility, the farm owner has the right to sell the horse to recover the board bill if the animal's owner defaults. A security interest should be a part of every boarding contract.

Sole proprietorship — A form of business in which a single person owns all the assets of the business and is liable for all the business debts.

Springing power of attorney — A power of attorney that comes into effect only when the principal becomes disabled.

Statute of limitations — A law that requires that legal action be taken with a specified period of time. If your state has a one-year statute of limitations for personal injury claims, for example, you must initiate legal action for such an injury within one year after the injury occurred, or within one year after you knew or should have known of the injury.

Title VII — Federal legislation that makes it illegal to discriminate against a person on the basis of race, color, religion, gender, or national origin.

Umbrella policy — A type of supplemental insurance policy that covers a wide range of possible sources of liability usually not addressed by a typical general liability policy.

Uniform Commercial Code (UCC) — A body of law that governs most commercial transactions, including the sales of horses. The UCC spells out in detail the rights and obligations of buyers and sellers.

Use tax — A state-imposed tax based on a percentage of the purchase price of items purchased elsewhere, then brought into the taxing state.

Will — A statement of how a person wishes his or her property to be distributed after death.

Worker's compensation — A state program for the protection of workers injured on the job. Under most worker's compensation programs, an injured worker can recover without having to prove fault on the part of his employer, but has no right to sue.

INDEX

RECOMMENDED READINGS

Toby, MC and Perch, KL. *Understanding Equine Law*. Lexington, KY: The Blood-Horse, Inc., 1999.

Newberry, JH Jr. *Legal Aspects of Horse Farm Operations* (2nd Ed.) Lexington, KY: University of Kentucky College of Law, Office of Continuing Education, 1995.

Equine Law Forms Compendium. Lexington, KY: University of Kentucky College of Law, Office of Continuing Education, 1999.

Proceedings of the University of Kentucky's Annual Equine Law Seminar (held annually in May). Lexington, KY: University of Kentucky College of Law, Office of Continuing Education.

Plank, TM and Plan, LR. *Accounting Desk Book* (11th Ed.) Paramus, NJ: Prentice Hall Press, 2000.

Low, RJ. *Bottom Line Basics*. Grants Pass OR : The Oasis Press, 1995.

Helpful business sites on the Internet

Service Corps of Retired Executives
—Counselors to America's Small Businesses
http://www.score.org

Small Business Administration
http://www.sba.gov

American Horse Council
http://www.horsecouncil.org

Miller, Griffin & Marks PSC — Equine Law.
Lexington, Kentucky-based law firm that concentrates
on equine law issues.
http://www.horselaw.com

Thoroughbred Owners and Breeders Association
http://www.toba.org

AQHA Online: The Official Site of the
American Quarter Horse Association.
http://www.aqha.org/information.html

American Association of Equine Practitioners
http://www.aaep.org

The Horse: Your Guide to Equine Health Care
http://www.thehorse.com

Picture Credits

Anne M. Eberhardt, 65-66, 68-72; Barbara D. Livingston, 67.
Odessa Chafin, 67.

EDITOR — JACQUELINE DUKE

ASSISTANT EDITOR — RENA BAER, JUDY L. MARCHMAN

COVER/BOOK DESIGN — SUZANNE C. DEPP

COVER PHOTO — ANNE M. EBERHARDT

About the Authors

Milton C. Toby, J.D., and Karen L. Perch, Ph.D., J.D., are partners in Perch & Toby, a law firm based in Lexington, Kentucky. Toby has enjoyed a lifelong involvement with horses, as an exhibitor of American Saddlebreds; as a competitor in hunter, combined training, and dressage events; as a steward for the American Horse Shows Association; as a director of the Kentucky Horse Council; as a journalist; and as a photographer. Toby and Perch are the authors of *Understanding Equine Law*, part of the Horse Health Care Library. He also is the author of *Col. Sager, Practitioner*, which recounts the experiences of the late Col. Floyd Sager, one of the country's most prominent equine veterinarians.

Milton C. Toby

Perch has extensive experience as a financial planner and counselor, and in estate planning, estate tax, and probate matters. She has authored numerous publications in those areas, and has appeared frequently as a guest on local television and radio programs. She also served on a United States Department of Agriculture-sponsored, multi-state research project involving farm family finances.

Karen L. Perch

The Horse Health Care Library

Other Titles in The Horse Health Care Library:

- Understanding EPM
- Understanding Equine First Aid
- Understanding the Equine Foot
- Understanding Equine Lameness
- Understanding Equine Nutrition
- Understanding Laminitis
- Understanding the Foal
- Understanding the Broodmare
- Understanding Horse Behavior
- Understanding Basic Horse Care
- Understanding the Older Horse

- Understanding the Stallion
- Understanding Breeding Management
- Understanding Equine Law
- Understanding the Young Horse
- Understanding the Equine Eye
- Understanding the Pony
- Understanding Equine Neurological Disorders
- The New Equine Sports Therapy
- Horse Theft Prevention Handbook

Videos from The Blood-Horse New Video Collection:
($39.95 each)

- Conformation: How to Buy a Winner
- Owning Thoroughbreds
- First Aid for Horses
- Lameness in the Horse

- Sales Preparation
- Insider's Guide to Buying at Auction
- The Expert's Guide to Buying Weanlings

To order call 800-582-5604
(In Kentucky call 859-278-2361)